CreAtive Chef 2

A blend of traditional and contemporary recipes for today's busy families.

Published by
The Tourette Syndrome Association, Inc.

The Tourette Syndrome Association is a national not for profit health organization dedicated to identifying the cause and controlling the effects of TS, and to finding its cure. A neurological condition characterized by involuntary body movements and uncontrollable vocalization, Tourette Syndrome generally first appears in childhood and persists throughout life.

All proceeds from the sale of Creative Chef 2 will be used to support TSA's programs of research, professional and public education, and individual and family services. Copies of Creative Chef 2 can be obtained by using the special tear-out order form at the back of the book, or by writing directly to:

Tourette Syndrome Association, Inc.
42-40 Bell Boulevard
Bayside, New York 11361
718-224-2999

First Printing   November, 1993   10,000 copies

Printed in the U.S.A.

FOR LAURIE

DAVID B. FINE

FOREWORD

In the fourteen years since the first Creative Chef, American culinary
arts have changed in important and often wonderful ways. The
nationalization of American regional cooking styles -- Cajun and South-
western come quickly to mind -- and the wide acceptance of many
international and ethnic cuisines have brought new delights to our
tables. Americans are also more keenly aware of health issues, but the
wider use of such ingredients as balsamic vinegar, Thai spices and
exotic peppers help ensure that healthier diets has not come at the
expense of tastiness.

This new edition of Creative Chef reflects these changes in American's
tastes and diets. In presenting this blend of the new and the traditional,
we offer something for all tastes. We have marked recipes that are
heart healthy with a "♥"; those that are easy and quick to prepare are
marked with a "🕐".

So enjoy - and Bon Appetit!

ACKNOWLEDGEMENTS

The Tourette Syndrome Association, Inc. wishes to express its gratitude to all those excellent cooks who generously shared their favorite recipes. Only the limitation of space and the need for balance prevented the inclusion of many more fine contributions. The names of all whose recipes appear here will be found at the back of this book.

As in the first edition of the _Creative Chef,_ the recipes were tested by the editors - to the delight of their families and friends. Of course, there is no such thing as a book of entirely new and original recipes and no claim for such is made.

The splendid cover and the artwork that introduces each new section were specially created for this book by David Fine, an artist and graphic designer in New York City.

Finally, our special thanks to the following businesses whose generous support helped make this book possible:

Aladdin Laminating, Inc., New York City
Bookbinders, Eatontown, NJ
Cedar West, New York City
Color by Pergament, New York City
Cutty Mounting and Finishing Co., Fairfield, NJ
Ecological Fibers, Lunenberg, MA
Hudson Printing, Inc., New York City
M & M Bindery, New York City
Panorama Press, Clifton, NJ
H.A.P.I., Elmhurst, NY
Harle Solomon, Flushing, NY

A very special thanks to the staff of the national Tourette Syndrome Association, Inc. for all their help in producing the final product.

TABLE OF CONTENTS

Appe-
tizers

DAVID B. FINE

AVOCADO MOUSSE

Serves 12

1 cup canned jellied beef consommé
2 teaspoons unflavored gelatin
3 ripe large avocados
8 ounces cream cheese, room temperature
Juice of 1 lemon

Garnish: Pesticide-free edible flowers (i.e., borage or citrus)
or lemon or lime slices

In a small saucepan, heat 1/2 cup of consommé over medium-high heat until melted. Remove from heat. Sprinkle gelatin over top of consommé and let stand until the gelatin is soft, about 5 minutes. Return to heat and stir until gelatin is dissolved, about 2 minutes. Set aside.

Pit, peel, and chop 2 of the avocados. Combine with remaining consommé and the cream cheese in a food processor or blender and purée until smooth. Blend in the reserved gelatin mixture. Turn the mixture into demitasse cups or cocktail glasses and chill until set, at least 4 hours, or as long as 24 hours. Alternatively, turn the mixture into a lightly oiled mold or bowl or into individual molds, smooth tops, cover tightly with plastic wrap, and refrigerate until set.

Just before serving, pit, peel and chop the remaining avocado. Dip the pieces briefly in lemon juice to keep them from darkening. To serve, garnish the top of each mousse with chopped avocado and edible flowers; serve with demitasse spoons for eating out of the cups or glasses. If using molds, dip the lower portion of the mold into a container of hot water for several seconds, then run a thin knife blade around the inside edge of the mold. Invert onto a serving plate or individual plates, garnish, and serve.

Variation: Instead of consommé, use chicken or vegetable stock and increase the amount of gelatin to 1 1/2 tablespoons.

APPETIZERS

CHICKEN TRIANGLES

Yield: 64

This dish is a quick and delicious variation of shrimp toast. Triangles can be frozen before cooking. Fry without thawing, allowing extra time to brown and heat thoroughly.

1 1/2 pounds skinned, boned chicken breasts, cut into 1-inch pieces
1 cup chopped scallions (green onions)
1 can (8 1/2 ounces) bamboo shoots, drained and coarsely chopped
2 large eggs, well beaten
1/4 cup cornstarch
1 teaspoon salt
16 slices firm white bread, crusts trimmed
Oil for frying

Put chicken, scallions and bamboo shoots in a blender or processor and process to consistency of paste. Blend in eggs, cornstarch and salt. Cut each bread slice into 4 triangles. Spread with chicken mixture. Refrigerate until ready to fry.

Heat 3/4 inch of oil in large skillet over medium-high heat. Add triangles face down and fry until golden brown, about 1 to 2 minutes. Serve hot.

Or, fry up to one hour before serving and keep warm in preheated 250° oven.

CHICK PEA HORS D'OEUVRES

Serves 6
♥

15 ounce can chick peas (garbanzos), drained and rinsed or
2 cups dry chick peas, soaked overnight and cooked until soft
(about 1 hour)
2 anchovy fillets, chopped or 1 tablespoon anchovy paste
1 clove garlic, minced
1 tablespoon capers
2 tablespoons finely chopped parsley
1/4 cup mayonnaise or olive oil

Combine all ingredients and chill.

CINNAMON-SUGAR COATED BLINTZES

Serves 8

These blintzes can be made ahead and frozen. Thaw before baking.

2 loaves (16 ounces each) soft white bread, crusts trimmed off
16 ounces cream cheese at room temperature
1 egg yolk
1/4 cup granulated sugar
1 stick (8 tablespoons) butter or margarine, melted
Cinnamon-sugar (mixture of cinnamon and granulated sugar)
Sour cream

Heat oven to 350°

Roll bread slices with a rolling pin until thin. Mix cream cheese, egg yolk
and sugar in a bowl until blended and smooth. Spread on bread. Roll up
each slice, jelly-roll style. Dip blintzes in melted butter then roll in cinnamon-
sugar to coat. Cut in half. Arrange on ungreased baking sheet and bake 10
to 15 minutes until golden brown.

Serve with sour cream.

ORIENTAL CHICKEN WINGS

Serves 20

11/2 *cups soy sauce*
3/4 cup dry sherry
1 cup Hoisin sauce
3/4 cup Chinese Plum sauce
16 minced scallions (green onions)
6 large cloves garlic, minced
1 large piece (1 inch) fresh ginger, peeled and minced
3/4 cup cider vinegar
1/2 cup honey
6 pounds chicken wings, tips trimmed

Combine all ingredients except chicken in a 3 quart saucepan. Bring to a boil and simmer 5 minutes. Disjoint wings and place in large container with cover. Pour cooked sauce over the wings. Cover and refrigerate overnight.

Heat oven to 375°.

Oil 2 large shallow roasting pans. Drain wings (saving sauce) and divide between pans. Bake uncovered for 1 to 1 1/2 hours, basting every 15 to 20 minutes with remaining sauce. Turn wings to brown evenly. Remove wings from pan and let cool. Wrap and refrigerate. Can be refrigerated for up to 3 days. Serve at room temperature.

SPICY CHICKEN WINGS

Serves 4

12 disjointed chicken wings, tips discarded
Salt and black pepper to taste
2 tablespoons peanut butter
2 tablespoons dark soy sauce
1 1/2 tablespoons honey
2 cloves garlic, crushed
1/4 to 1/2 teaspoon crushed hot dried peppers

Garnish: 1/3 cup finely chopped roasted and salted peanuts
     Big handful of fresh chopped cilantro

Heat oven to 400°

Put wings in a single layer in a baking dish. Salt and pepper to taste and bake for 30 minutes, or until they begin to brown.

Combine peanut butter, soy sauce, honey, garlic and hot peppers in saucepan over low heat, stirring until well blended.

Spoon or brush the peanut sauce over chicken. Return to the oven and bake 10 to 15 minutes. Do not allow the sauce to burn.

Remove chicken from the oven and sprinkle with peanuts and cilantro. Cool slightly before serving.

STUFFED BAKED CLAMS

Serves 6

Use cherrystone shells for stuffing.

11/2 dozen fresh clams, 9 cherrystone and 9 chowder
1/2 cup olive oil
3 cloves garlic, peeled and quartered
2 tablespoons parsley
About 1/2 cup dry bread crumbs

Heat oven to 350°

Open clams by steaming them briefly in 1 inch boiling water. Remove clams from shells and save the juice. Put clams, 1/4 cup reserved juice, the oil, garlic and parsley in blender. Blend briefly so clams are not chopped too fine.

Pour mixture into a bowl and stir in bread crumbs. Let sit a few minutes until crumbs absorb moisture. Fill shells. Place on baking sheet and bake 30 minutes or until lightly browned. Serve hot.

CHRISTOPHER'S ALIEN EYEBALLS

Perfect for Halloween (or any child's party).

1 package Ritz crackers
1 container spreadable cheddar cheese
1 jar Pimiento stuffed green olives

Spread cheese on crackers and top with one half an olive, sliced in half so it looks like a green eye with a red pupil.

CRABMEAT & ARTICHOKES IN PITA

Serves a crowd

Spicy party starters.

1 large green pepper chopped into 1/2 inch pieces
1 tablespoon vegetable oil
2 packages frozen artichoke hearts thawed, or 2 (14 ounce) cans
*   artichoke hearts, drained and chopped*
1 1/2 cups mayonnaise
3 scallions (green onions) thinly sliced
1 cup freshly grated Parmesan cheese
1 teaspoon lemon juice
4 teaspoons Worcestershire sauce
4 pickled jalapeño peppers (optional)
1 teaspoon celery salt
1 pound fresh crabmeat, cleaned, or 1 package frozen crabmeat,
*   thawed, drained and cleaned*
1/3 cup slivered almonds

Heat oven to 375°

Sauté green pepper in oil over medium heat until soft. Let cool. In food processor or blender combine green pepper, artichokes, mayonnaise, scallions, Parmesan cheese, lemon juice, Worcestershire sauce, jalapeño peppers and celery salt. Mix well, but leave chunky. Gently stir in crabmeat. Transfer to buttered oven-proof dish. Sprinkle with almonds. Bake for 25 to 30 minutes until top is golden and mixture is bubbly. Serve with pita triangles.

APPETIZERS

HOT CRAB DIP

Serve with crackers or warm pita wedges.

8 ounce package cream cheese at room temperature
1 tablespoon milk
1 teaspoon Worcestershire sauce
1 or 2 dashes Tabasco sauce
1 can (6 1/2 ounces) crabmeat, drained and flaked
1 cup (4 ounces) Cheddar cheese, shredded

Heat oven to 350°

Mix cream cheese, milk, Worcestershire and Tabasco until smooth and well blended. Stir in crabmeat. Spoon into a small casserole and sprinkle cheese on top. Bake 20 to 25 minutes or until cheese bubbles.

CRABMEAT SPREAD

2 tablespoons chopped onion
1 clove garlic, minced
3 tablespoons butter
1/4 cup flour
1/4 cup dry sherry wine
3/4 cup heavy cream
1/4 cup chili sauce
1 teaspoon Tabasco sauce
1 can crabmeat, about 12 ounces, drained and flaked
4 slices American cheese, cut up

Heat oven to 350°

Brown onion and minced garlic in butter in a large skillet. Take off heat and blend in flour. Add sherry, cream, chili and Tabasco. Cook until mixture thickens.

Add crabmeat and cheese. Stir until cheese melts. Place in a crock and bake for 20 minutes. Serve hot.

8

CRAB CROSTINI

Serves 8

The crabmeat mixture can be made several hours ahead and refrigerated.

8 ounces lump crabmeat
1/2 cup diced red bell pepper
2 tablespoons plus 2 teaspoons reduced-calorie mayonnaise
2 tablespoons chopped fresh parsley
1 tablespoon chopped fresh chives
1 tablespoon fresh lime juice
1 tablespoon Dijon mustard
2 teaspoons grated Parmesan cheese
4 to 5 drops hot pepper sauce
1 loaf Italian bread, cut into 16 slices

Preheat broiler. Line broiler pan with foil. Pick over the crabmeat to remove any cartilage.

In a medium bowl, combine the crabmeat, bell pepper, mayonnaise, parsley, chives, lime juice, mustard, Parmesan cheese and hot pepper sauce. Blend well.

Spread 1 tablespoon of the crab mixture on each slice of bread. Place on broiler pan and broil 4 inches from the heat for 5 to 6 minutes, or until lightly browned.

APPETIZERS

BEEF EMPAÑADAS

Yield: 12-15

Pastry
2 cups flour
1/2 teaspoon salt
1/2 cup (1 stick) cold unsalted butter, cut into small cubes
3 tablespoons vegetable shortening
5 tablespoons cold water (approximate)

Filling
1 small onion, chopped
2 cloves garlic, chopped
3 tablespoons olive oil
1/2 pound ground beef
1 1/2 teaspoons dried oregano
1 tablespoon paprika
2 tablespoons cumin
Dash cinnamon
Cayenne pepper to taste
1 cup water

Pastry: Combine flour and salt. Cut in the butter and shortening until the texture of crumbs. Add the water, one tablespoon at a time. Mix to form a soft dough. Do not overmix. Chill 1 hour.

Filling: Heat olive oil in a sauté pan. Add onion and garlic and cook over medium heat until soft and translucent. Add meat, crumble with back of fork. Season with herbs and spices. Brown the meat and then add a cup of water. Cook over low heat until dry. Cover and refrigerate until well chilled.

Heat oven to 375°

Roll dough into long cylinder, approximately 2 inches in diameter. Cut dough into equal-size pieces. Roll out each piece into rounds, approximately 4 inches in diameter. Brush outer edge lightly with water. Place 1 tablespoon filling in center. Fold round in half, forming a semicircle. Pinch edges together. Press with tines of fork to seal. Transfer to greased cookie sheet. Repeat with remaining dough and filling. Bake until golden, about 30 minutes.

GUACAMOLE DIP

Serves 6

For guacamole with more body, reserve half of the avocado. Mash it with a fork, then add it to the blended mixture.

2 medium-size ripe avocados
1/4 cup fresh lemon juice
2 garlic cloves, crushed
1/4 cup chopped sweet Spanish onion
1/2 cup sour cream

Peel the avocados, remove the pits and chop coarsely. Put all ingredients in a blender or food processor. Process on low to medium speed until smooth, stopping to scrape down the sides as necessary. Spoon into a serving dish. If desired, chill, tightly covered, before serving. (Stir before serving if the top of the dip has darkened.) Serve with tortilla chips or raw vegetables.

CHEESE-TOPPED MUSHROOM CAPS AND SPINACH

Serves 4

8 very large mushrooms
2 tablespoons butter
1/4 cup minced onion
1/4 cup grated carrots
1 cup packed spinach leaves, chopped
2 tablespoons sunflower seeds
1 tablespoon minced fresh parsley
1 teaspoon Worcestershire sauce
2 tablespoons shredded Gruyère or Swiss cheese

Carefully trim stems from mushroom caps. Chop stems. Melt the butter in a medium-size skillet. Add the mushroom caps and cook until they give up their liquid and it evaporates. Remove the mushrooms to a plate.

Put onions, carrots and spinach in the skillet and sauté over low heat, stirring constantly, until the spinach is wilted and any excess water evaporates. Remove from heat.

Process sunflower seeds in a blender using on/off switch until completely ground. Stir into the spinach mixture, along with the parsley and Worcestershire.

Stuff the mushroom caps with spinach mixture. Top with cheese. Cover and refrigerate until ready to serve.

When ready to serve, place stuffed mushrooms in a shallow baking dish and bake at 350° until cheese melts. Serve hot.

OYSTERS ROCKEFELLER

Serves 5

Cherrystone clams can also be used for this dish.

3/4 cup scallions (green onions), chopped
1 celery rib, chopped
1 garlic clove, peeled and chopped
3 tablespoons butter
1/3 cup fresh parsley, chopped
11/2 cups fresh spinach, washed and chopped
1 teaspoon Pernod
2 teaspoons lemon juice
3 dashes Tabasco sauce
1/4 cup bread crumbs
Dash of Worcestershire sauce
2 tablespoons Parmesan cheese
1/2 teaspoon salt
1/4 teaspoon pepper
4 tablespoons butter, melted
30 fresh oysters, drained

Sauté scallions, celery and garlic in 3 tablespoons butter until soft. Stir in parsley and spinach, and cook until spinach wilts. Put in blender and add Pernod and lemon juice. Purée until creamy.

Transfer to a bowl and mix in Tabasco sauce, bread crumbs, Worcestershire sauce, Parmesan cheese, salt and pepper. Mix in remaining butter.

Place oysters in 5 small oven-proof dishes and spread a layer of sauce over them. Put in a very hot oven or broiler for 10 minutes, or until topping is golden brown. Serve immediately.

SALMON CHEESECAKE

Serves 10

1 cup plain cracker crumbs
41/2 tablespoons melted butter
16 ounce bar cream cheese, broken up
3 large eggs
3/4 cup sour cream
8 ounces canned salmon, drained, skinned, deboned and flaked
Juice of 1/2 small lemon, or to taste
1/4 cup minced white onion
Salt and black pepper to taste
11/2 teaspoons dried dillweed, or to taste

Garnish: Fresh dill sprigs
    Crusty French bread, cut up

Heat oven to 350°

Combine the crumbs and butter. Press into an 81/2 inch springform pan. Bake for 10 to 15 minutes, or until lightly browned. Take pan out of oven and set aside.

Combine the cream cheese, eggs and 1/4 cup of the sour cream in a food processor or blender. Pour into bowl. Add all remaining ingredients except balance of sour cream and mix well. Adjust seasonings as desired. Pour over the crust. Bake at same temperature for 50 minutes or until the center is only slightly wobbly when touched. The top will crack and brown - do not worry. Remove cheesecake from the pan. Cool completely. Remove the bottom of pan and place on a serving plate.

Spread remaining sour cream over the top. Refrigerate for at least 2 hours, or until completely chilled. Just before serving, garnish the top with the dill sprigs. Serve in wedges, passing the warmed bread separately.

SALMON MOUSSE

Yield: One quart mold

This recipe freezes well in a mold. Defrost before unmolding. Serve with crackers, cucumber slices or party rye bread.

1 envelope unflavored gelatin
2 tablespoons lemon juice
1 small onion, sliced
1/2 cup boiling water
1/2 cup mayonnaise
1/4 teaspoon paprika
2 tablespoons bottled white horseradish
1 teaspoon dried dill or 1 tablespoon chopped fresh dill
1 can (16 ounces) salmon, drained and flaked
1 cup heavy cream

Empty gelatin into blender or food processor. Add lemon juice, onion and boiling water. Process at high speed. Add mayonnaise, paprika, horse-radish, dill and salmon. Process at high speed. Add cream slowly while blending. Pour into 1 quart mold and chill till set. Unmold just before serving.

SHRIMP WITH ROQUEFORT-SCENTED BUTTER

Serves 6

1 pound large or jumbo shrimp, unpeeled
1/2 cup dry white wine
1 shallot, chopped
1 sprig parsley
4 tablespoons mayonnaise
1 tablespoon Roquefort cheese
Dash Tabasco

Garnish: Parsley, chervil or chives

Place the shrimp, wine, shallot and parsley in a saucepan. Add 1/2 cup water and bring to a boil. Simmer until shrimp are cooked, about 5 minutes. Remove the shrimp and boil the liquid until it reduces to about 1/4 cup. Strain the liquid and set aside.

Meanwhile, peel and devein the shrimp and arrange them on six appetizer plates.

Add the mayonnaise, cheese and Tabasco to the reduced and strained cooking liquid. Spoon this sauce over the shrimp and garnish the plates with parsley, chervil or chives. Serve at room temperature.

SHRIMP STUFFED FRENCH BREAD

Yield: 1 loaf

May be made one day in advance.

1 loaf French bread
6 ounces cream cheese
1 small can shrimp (about 6 ounces), drained
2 tablespoons sour cream
1 teaspoon Worcestershire sauce
1 tablespoon chopped fresh dill or 1 teaspoon dried dill
Salt to taste
3/4 cup butter (6 tablespoons) softened
1/3 cup chopped scallions (green onions)

Cut loaf of bread in half lengthwise. Scoop soft dough from top and bottom of loaf leaving a shell.

Mix together cream cheese, shrimp, sour cream, Worcestershire, dill and salt. Fill top half of loaf with this mixture.

Mix butter and onions. Spread this mixture on bottom layer. Place the halves together and wrap in foil. Refrigerate several hours. Slice thin to serve.

APPETIZERS

SPANAKOPITA (SPINACH CHEESE TRIANGLES)

Yield: 44

These multilayered pastries filled with spinach and cheese can be made and refrigerated or frozen ahead of time, then baked just before serving. The secret to their triangular shape is folding them just like a flag.

2 large eggs
1 medium size onion, quartered
8 ounces feta cheese, crumbled
8 ounces cream cheese, room temperature
1 package (10 ounces) frozen chopped spinach, thawed and
*   squeezed dry*
2 tablespoons chopped fresh parsley
1 tablespoon chopped fresh dill or 1 teaspoon dillweed
Dash pepper
2 packages phyllo or strudel leaves
2 sticks (1 cup) butter or margarine, melted

Whirl eggs, onion and feta cheese in blender until smooth. Add cream cheese; whirl until smooth. Add spinach, parsley, dill and pepper and blend just until combined. Refrigerate at least 1 hour.

Stack 2 leaves (16 x 22 inches each) phyllo pastry on work surface. Cover rest with plastic wrap to prevent drying. For each triangle cut off a strip 2 inches wide and 16 inches long, cutting through both leaves. Brush with melted butter. Place a rounded teaspoon of filling on one end of strip. Fold one corner to opposite side, forming a triangle. Continue folding keeping triangle shape, to the other end.

Arrange filled pastries on ungreased jelly-roll pan. (I use large oven liner pans and turn the edges up.) Repeat with remaining pastry and filling.

Heat oven to 375°. Bake for 20 minutes or until golden brown. Serve hot.

FETTUNTA WITH SPINACH

Serves 4

8 slices coarse-textured, crusty Italian bread, 1/2-inch thick
2 pounds fresh spinach or 10 ounces frozen spinach leaves
1/4 cup olive oil
2 cloves garlic, finely chopped
2 tablespoons finely chopped sun-dried tomatoes, drained of oil
Salt and freshly ground pepper

Heat oven to 400°

Cut the bread slices and set aside. It is OK if they get a little dry.

Wash, dry and remove the stems of the fresh spinach. Put the spinach in a large saucepan with 1 cup water and a pinch of salt. Cook the spinach for two to three minutes, just until soft. (If using frozen spinach, boil it until it is soft.) When the spinach is cooked, drain and squeeze out all excess water.

Brush the bread slices with some of the olive oil, arrange them in a single layer on a baking sheet and bake until they are golden, about five minutes.

Meanwhile, heat the remaining oil in a skillet over medium heat. Cook the garlic and tomatoes for one to two minutes, then add spinach and salt and pepper to taste. Cook and stir the mixture for two to three minutes. Season to taste.

Let the mixture cool for a few minutes, then spread on the toast slices and serve.

APPETIZERS

TAPAS (Spanish Potato Tortilla)

Serves 8

Tortilla
3/4 cup olive oil
3 large potatoes, peeled and sliced 1/4 inch
2 teaspoons salt
1 large onion, thinly sliced
1 red bell pepper, cored and sliced into thin rings
4 large eggs
Fresh ground pepper

Heat olive oil in a 10-12 inch sauté pan until hot. Add potato slices, one at a time, so they do not stick together. Season with salt. Turn the potatoes to coat with oil. Continue to cook on medium-high heat until potatoes start to brown. Add the onion and bell pepper and reduce heat to medium. Cook until everything is tender, approximately 7 to 8 minutes. Transfer to a colander set over a bowl. Drain off oil and reserve. Sprinkle with salt.

Beat the eggs in a mixing bowl and add a little salt and pepper. Stir in potato mixture. Heat 3 tablespoons of reserved oil in a non-stick sauté pan. Pour mixture in and distribute the potatoes evenly around the pan. Cook over medium heat 2 minutes. Shake the pan to prevent sticking. When the tortilla is firm, but not dry, invert it onto a plate. Slide it back into the pan to brown the other side. Heat on medium until second side is cooked. Slide it out onto cutting board and cut into wedges or squares. Serve at room temperature or warm, as is or with red sauce (below).

Red Sauce
1 tablespoon olive oil
1 medium onion, chopped
1 medium tomato chopped
1/2 cup water
Saffron (a few strands)
1/2 cup roasted red bell peppers, chopped

Heat oil in small saucepan. Sauté the onion and garlic over medium heat until translucent. Add tomato, water, saffron, salt and pepper to taste. Simmer 20 minutes. Add bell peppers. Simmer another 10 minutes. Turn up heat to medium-high and reduce sauce to fairly thick consistency. Adjust seasoning to taste.

SIRLOIN TERIYAKI

Serves 12

1 pound top sirloin, cut into 48 1/2-inch cubes
1 can unsweetened mandarin orange sections
3/4 cup soy sauce

Alternate 4 pieces of meat with 4 mandarin orange sections on small skewers or bamboo picks. Arrange in single layer in shallow pan. Pour soy sauce over the skewers. Cover and marinate 1 hour in refrigerator, turning several times. Place in broiler pan and broil to desired doneness. Arrange on serving platter.

KAMINARI DOFU (TOFU SIDE DISH)

Serves 4

♥

From Gochiso-sama -- a culinary newsletter from Japan.

2 blocks momen (cotton) style tofu
4 tablespoons sesame oil
4 tablespoons low-sodium soy sauce

<u>*Garnish*</u>
1/2 cup grated and drained daikon (white radish)
1/2 cup minced green onions (scallions)
Togarashi or minced dried red pepper to taste
Wasabi horseradish to taste

Place the tofu between 2 plates and leave for 20 to 30 minutes. Drain off excess water and mash tofu between your fingers in a bowl.

Heat the oil in a wok. Add tofu and stir quickly. Add soy sauce and continue cooking over high heat for a few minutes.

To serve: place the tofu mixture in individual bowls, top with grated daikon. Sprinkle generously with green onions. Sprinkle with red pepper and place a dab of wasabi in the center. Serve piping hot.

ZUCCHINI PANCAKES WITH SALSA

Yield: 8-10 3" Pancakes

Same batter makes muffins. Fill muffin cups 2/3 full and bake at 425° for 20-25 minutes.

3/4 cup sifted flour
21/2 teaspoons baking powder
1 tablespoon sugar
11/4 cups yellow cornmeal
3/4 teaspoon salt
1 egg
1 cup milk
2 tablespoons oil
1 cup grated zucchini
3 tablespoons finely chopped onion
Salsa

Stir together flour, baking powder, sugar, cornmeal and salt in medium bowl. In separate bowl, mix egg, milk, oil, zucchini and onion. Pour over dry ingredients and lightly stir until just barely moist.

Grease and heat skillet or griddle. Cook 2 or 3 pancakes at a time over medium heat until both sides are golden brown and insides are firm. Serve with Salsa.

DELICIOUS CRABMEAT PIE

Makes 1 9-inch pie

1 9-inch pie shell
2 tablespoons minced scallions (green onions)
3 tablespoons butter or margarine
1 cup fresh or frozen crabmeat, cleaned and flaked
Salt and pepper to taste
2 tablespoons white wine or vermouth
3 eggs
1 cup heavy cream
1 tablespoon tomato paste
1/4 cup grated Swiss or Jarlsberg cheese

Heat oven to 375°

Bake the pie shell for 5 minutes and allow it to cool. In a skillet, over low heat, cook the scallions in butter until they are soft, then add the crabmeat and stir. Sprinkle in the salt, pepper and the wine. Raise the heat and boil for 1 minute, then allow mixture to cool until it is lukewarm.

Meanwhile, beat the eggs with the cream and tomato paste. Gradually add to the lukewarm mixture. Add the grated cheese. Pour this into the cooled pie shell and bake for 35 to 40 minutes.

NOTES

COCONUT BREAD

Yield: 1 loaf

2 cups plus extra all-purpose flour
Pinch salt
1/2 tablespoon baking powder
8 ounces shredded coconut
6 tablespoons granulated sugar
1/3 cup plus 2 tablespoons raisins
1 egg, beaten
1/2 cup plus 2 tablespoons evaporated milk
1/4 cup butter or margarine
1 teaspoon vanilla extract
1/4 cup unsalted chopped nuts (optional)

Glaze
1 tablespoon granulated sugar
1 tablespoon hot water

Heat oven to 350°

Grease and flour a loaf pan. In large bowl, mix together flour, salt, baking powder, coconut, sugar and raisins. Add egg, evaporated milk, butter and vanilla; mix well. Add nuts, if using. Batter will be sticky and heavy. Pour batter into prepared loaf pan, smoothing top with back of spoon dipped lightly in hot water.

To make glaze, combine 1 tablespoon sugar and 1 tablespoon hot water and brush over top of loaf. Bake 40 minutes or until toothpick inserted in center comes out clean. Let cool and turn out onto wire rack. Cut in thick slices and serve warm or at room temperature.

CORN BREAD

Serves 20

2 1/2 *cups refined yellow cornmeal*
2 1/3 *cups whole wheat pastry flour*
1 tablespoon baking powder
2/3 teaspoon salt
2 1/2 *cups milk*
4 eggs, beaten
2/3 cup oil
1/3 cup honey

Heat oven to 350°

Mix dry ingredients together in a large mixing bowl. Mix wet ingredients in a second bowl, then pour wet mixture into dry ingredients. Stir briefly, but do not beat out all the lumps.

Grease a 10 x 14 inch baking pan. Bake in oven for 30-35 minutes until golden brown and firm to the touch.

CRACKED PEPPER AND PARMESAN CHEESE BREAD

Yield: 2 loaves

1 tablespoon sugar
11/4 cups warm water
1 package active dry yeast
31/2 to 4 cups all-purpose flour
2 teaspoons coarsely crushed peppercorns (measured after crushing)
3/4 cup grated Parmesan cheese
1/4 cup bottled Ranch dressing
1 teaspoon salt

Dissolve sugar in 1/4 cup warm water; add yeast and stir to dissolve. Set aside and let mixture get foamy. Put 21/2 cups of the flour in a large bowl, adding 1 cup warm water followed by the yeast mixture. Mix well, cover and set aside for about 1 hour.

Beat dough down. Add remaining ingredients and enough additional flour to make a workable dough. Knead on floured surface 10 minutes until smooth. Place in a greased bowl, cover and let dough double in size. Punch down, place on lightly floured surface and let rest about 10 minutes. Divide in half, form each into a loaf and place in two greased bread pans. Cover and let rise about 45 minutes.

Heat oven to 350°. Bake breads for 40 to 50 minutes. Cool 10 minutes then invert on wire rack. Cool breads on rack.

27

BREADS

DATE NUT BREAD

Yield: 2 loaves

3/4 cup chopped nuts
1 cup pitted dates, chopped
1 1/2 teaspoons baking soda
1/2 teaspoon salt
3/4 cup water
1/4 cup butter or margarine
3 eggs
1/2 teaspoon vanilla extract
1 cup sugar
1 1/2 cups all-purpose flour

Heat oven to 350°

Mix together the nuts, dates, baking soda and salt in a bowl. Boil water and add margarine until melted. Add to date and nut mixture and let stand at least 15 minutes.

Beat the eggs with vanilla. Stir in the sugar and then the flour. Add to the date mixture. Bake in greased loaf pans for about 1 hour (less, if you use small loaf pans).

PEPPERONI BREAD

Yield: 8-10 wedges

Bread can be served warm or cold.

1 loaf frozen white bread dough, thawed
1 pound pepperoni, thinly sliced
8 ounces (2 cups) shredded mozzarella cheese
1/4 cup grated Parmesan cheese
Oregano
Black pepper
Garlic powder to taste
1 egg white, beaten

Heat oven to 375°

Cut thawed bread dough loaf in half. Form each half into a ball and roll out dough, one ball at a time, into a circle, to fit on a 12 x 18 inch cookie sheet. Top with sliced pepperoni, then the shredded mozzarella cheese. Sprinkle with grated Parmesan cheese, then the seasonings to taste.

Roll out second ball of dough, same size as first, and place over pepperoni cheese spread. Pinch edges of lower and upper layers of dough together to seal. Brush upper layer with egg white.

Bake for 25 to 30 minutes or until top is golden brown. Let cool for 10 to 15 minutes before serving.

BREADS

POPOVERS

Serves 6

1 cup sifted all-purpose white flour
1/2 teaspoon salt
2 large eggs, room temperature
1 cup milk
Melted unsalted butter for brushing the popover pan(s)

Heat oven to 400°

Sift the flour and salt into a bowl. In another bowl, beat the eggs and milk. Add milk mixture to flour mixture and stir until smooth. Place large custard cups or muffin tins in oven for 5 minutes. Take out and brush liberally with the melted butter. Fill cups/tins half full with batter and bake for 20 minutes. Turn heat down to 350° and bake an additional 10 minutes or until popovers are golden brown. Serve immediately.

PUMPKIN BREAD

Yield: 2 loaves

This recipe is over 200 years old. It can also be baked in muffin cups (but be sure to reduce baking time).

3 cups granulated sugar
1 cup vegetable oil
3 1/2 cups all-purpose flour
1 teaspoon ground cinnamon
2/3 cup water
2 teaspoons baking soda
2 cups cooked or canned pumpkin
1 cup chopped pecans
1 1/2 teaspoons ground nutmeg
4 large eggs
1 cup golden raisins

Heat oven to 350°

Grease and flour 2 loaf pans.

Mix sugar and oil. Add all other ingredients; mix well. Pour into loaf pans. Bake 1 hour or until toothpick inserted in middle comes out clean. Invert on rack and cool.

BREADS

REAL ITALIAN BREAD

Yield: 2 loaves

1 cup semolina
4 cups all-purpose flour
1 tablespoon salt
13/4 cups warm water
1 envelope active dry yeast, softened in 1/4 cup warm water

In a large bowl, sift 1 cup semolina with 2 cups flour. Add salt and mix. Add warm water, mix well. Add yeast mixture and blend thoroughly. Add enough additional flour to make a workable dough. Knead well. Place on lightly floured surface and allow to rest 5 to 10 minutes. Knead again, 5 to 8 minutes.

Place dough in lightly greased bowl, cover and let rise until doubled in size. Punch down, place on lightly floured surface and divide in two. Roll each half to form long, slender loaves. Place on greased cookie sheet or Italian bread loaf pan. Cover with towel and let dough double in size.

Heat oven to 425°. Bake for 10 minutes, reduce temperature to 350°, and bake 45 to 55 minutes longer until golden brown. Cool on rack.

ZUCCHINI BREAD

Yield: 2 loaves

This recipe freezes well. Makes two large loaves.

2 cups grated unpeeled zucchini
2 cups sugar
1 cup vegetable oil
3 eggs, beaten until light and frothy
2 teaspoons vanilla extract
3 cups flour
1 teaspoon baking soda
1 teaspoon salt
1/2 teaspoon cinnamon
1 cup chopped nuts
1/2 teaspoon grated lemon rind (optional)
1 cup raisins

Heat oven to 350°

Drain zucchini well and combine with sugar, oil, eggs and vanilla in a large bowl. Sift flour, soda, salt and cinnamon together and add to zucchini mixture. Blend well. Stir in nuts, raisins and lemon rind (if desired). Divide batter between two well-greased 8 x 5 x 3 inch loaf pans.

Bake 70 minutes or until toothpick inserted in center comes out clean. Cool in pan or cool slightly and remove to wire rack to cool thoroughly.

BEST BLUEBERRY MUFFINS WITH OATS

Yield: 16 muffins

You may use unsweetened frozen berries if fresh are not in season, but you will have to extend baking time.

1/2 stick (4 tablespoons) butter or margarine
1/4 cup vegetable oil
1 cup milk
2 eggs slightly beaten or (use 1 yolk and 2 whites)
3/4 cup granulated sugar
1 cup whole-wheat flour
1 cup all-purpose flour
*1 cup oat flour ***
4 teaspoons baking powder
1/2 teaspoon salt
1/2 teaspoon ground cinnamon
1 cup blueberries

Topping
2 tablespoons sugar
1/4 teaspoon cinnamon

Heat oven to 375°

Spray muffin cups with vegetable cooking spray. Heat butter and oil until butter melts. Add milk, then add beaten eggs. In separate bowl, mix sugar with other dry ingredients. Combine wet and dry ingredients. Stir quickly and lightly until flour is moist. Stir in blueberries.

Spoon batter into muffin cups, filling slightly more than half full. Mix sugar and cinnamon together for topping and sprinkle over muffins.

Bake 20 to 25 minutes or until toothpick inserted in center comes out clean.

*Oat flour is made by placing 1 to 2 cups of oats into food processor or blender. Process until granular.

LEMON-POPPY SEED MUFFINS

Yield: 12 muffins

Batter can be made the night before, covered tightly and refrigerated. Allow batter to come to room temperature before spooning into muffin tins; bake according to directions.

Muffins
6 tablespoons unsalted butter at room temperature
6 tablespoons shortening
1 cup sugar
2 eggs
2/3 cup milk
1/3 cup lemon juice
3 cups all-purpose flour
4 teaspoons salt
1/4 cup poppy seeds
4 teaspoons grated lemon rind

Glaze (optional)
2 cups powdered sugar
1/4 cup lemon juice
1 teaspoon vanilla extract

Heat oven to 350°

Muffins: Grease 12 (3") muffin-pan cups. Cream together butter, shortening and sugar. In another bowl, beat together eggs, milk and lemon juice. Mix together flour, baking powder, and salt in third bowl. Alternately add wet and dry ingredients to butter-sugar mixture. Stir in poppy seeds and lemon rind. Divide batter among the 12 muffin cups. Bake for 25 minutes.

Glaze: While muffins are baking, combine powdered sugar, lemon juice and vanilla in small bowl. When muffins are done, let sit a minute, then turn out onto wire racks. Cool about 10 minutes, dip each muffin into glaze and set back on rack placed over a sheet of wax paper. Drizzle any remaining glaze over muffin tops.

Variation: Substitute 1/2 cup finely chopped walnuts for poppy seeds.

35

OLD-FASHIONED BRAN MUFFINS

Yield: 24 muffins

These muffins freeze very well and may be reheated in oven at low temperature or in microwave on Defrost.

2 cups unprocessed whole bran
2 cups whole-wheat flour
2 tablespoons, plus 1 teaspoon baking powder
1 teaspoon salt
1/2 cup packed brown sugar
1/2 cup granulated sugar
1 tablespoon ground cinnamon
1 tablespoon ground nutmeg (optional)
2 large eggs
2 cups milk
6 tablespoons molasses
6 tablespoons vegetable oil
1/2 cup raisins

Heat oven to 425°

Mix first 8 ingredients in a large bowl. Add remaining ingredients and mix thoroughly. Spoon into paper-lined muffin cups. Bake 12 to 15 minutes.

OATMEAL BISCUITS

Yield: 12

1 3/4 cups all-purpose flour
1/3 cup rolled oats (or plain oatmeal)
1/4 teaspoon salt
1/2 teaspoon cinnamon
2 teaspoons sugar
1 teaspoon baking powder
1/2 teaspoon baking soda
5 tablespoons chilled butter
3/4 cup buttermilk

Heat oven to 400°

In a bowl, combine the dry ingredients. Cut in the chilled butter with a pastry blender or your fingertips until the mixture resembles coarse meal. Pour in the buttermilk and mix well to make a soft dough. Turn dough out on a floured board and knead it two or three times.

Roll out the dough 1/2-inch thick and cut into 3-inch rounds. Transfer to a greased and floured baking sheet. Bake the biscuits for 15 to 20 minutes, or until tops are golden.

SOUPS SALADS SAUCES

DAVID B. FINE

NOTES

CLASSIC CUBAN BEAN SOUP

Serves 4 to 6

1 pound dried black beans
2 quarts water
2 tablespoons salt
2 cloves garlic
1/2 tablespoon cumin
1/2 tablespoon oregano
1 teaspoon white vinegar
1/2 cup olive oil
1 very large onion, finely chopped
1 green pepper, finely chopped

Marinade
3 cups cooked rice
1 large onion, chopped
1/4 cup olive oil or to taste
3 tablespoons white vinegar

In a covered pot, soak beans in water overnight. Next day, add salt and boil the beans until they are soft. In a bowl, crush together the garlic cloves, cumin, oregano and vinegar and set them aside.

Marinade: Combine all ingredients and marinate a few hours (not in refrigerator).

In a Dutch oven, heat the olive oil, add the onion and pepper and sauté them until the onion is soft and golden. Then add the crushed ingredients and cook slowly over a low flame for a few minutes. Add the soaked beans to the Dutch oven and cook slowly approximately 40 to 50 minutes.

Before serving, add a scoop of the rice marinade to each bowl of soup.

COLD TOMATO, BASIL AND WALNUT SOUP

Serves 6

6 to 8 fresh tomatoes, peeled and cored or 2 (35-ounce) cans
Italian whole tomatoes, drained
1/4 cup minced fresh basil
2 to 3 tablespoons walnut oil
1 to 2 tablespoons balsamic vinegar
Salt and pepper to taste
1/2 cup toasted walnuts, chopped
Small basil sprigs

Purée tomatoes in blender or food processor. Add all remaining ingredients to tomatoes except walnuts and basil sprigs. Mix to blend. Adjust seasonings, oil and vinegar to taste.

Cover and refrigerate, if possible, for 3 hours. Ladle into bowls and garnish with walnuts and basil sprigs.

CREAM OF LEEK SOUP

Yield: 2 1/2 quarts

This lovely Welsh soup has a delicate flavor.

1/4 cup (1/2 stick) unsalted butter
2 pounds leeks (white and light green parts only), coarsely chopped
3 medium yellow onions, coarsely chopped
2 large celery stalks, chopped
1 small russet potato, peeled and coarsely chopped
6 cups rich beef stock
1/4 cup minced fresh parsley
1/2 teaspoon freshly grated nutmeg
1/2 cup (or more) whipping cream
Salt and freshly ground pepper
Additional freshly grated nutmeg (optional)

Melt butter in heavy large saucepan over low heat. Add leeks, onions, celery and potato and cook until tender and golden brown, stirring occasionally, about 20 minutes. Add stock, parsley and nutmeg. Cover and simmer 1 hour or until thickened.

Purée soup in batches in blender or food processor. Return to saucepan. Mix in 1/2 cup cream. Stir until heated through. Season with salt and pepper. Ladle soup into bowls. Top each with cream and nutmeg, if desired.

41

QUICK CREAM OF SPINACH SOUP

Serves 6 to 8

🕐

3 medium potatoes, peeled and chopped
3 tablespoons dry white wine
1 medium onion, peeled and chopped
5 cups chicken stock
1 pound fresh spinach, soaked in water for two hours, washed,
     drained and chopped (roots discarded)
Salt and pepper to taste
Pinch nutmeg
1/2 to 1 teaspoon paprika
Pinch of cayenne pepper
4 ounces heavy cream

Garnish: Parmesan cheese or chopped egg

In a large soup pot, add potatoes, white wine and onion to chicken stock; cook until potatoes are soft. Add spinach and cook briefly - just until spinach wilts. Purée all in food processor or blender, leaving spinach in small pieces (or first purée potatoes and onion, then purée spinach separately).

Return soup to pot and season with salt, pepper, nutmeg, paprika and cayenne pepper. Just before serving, add cream and reheat, but do not boil. Garnish with Parmesan cheese, chopped hard-boiled egg, or leave unadorned.

FISH SOUP WITH CROSTINI

Serves 4

This version of Zuppa di Pesce is delicious with or without a pinch of saffron.

5-6 threads saffron (optional)
1/4 cup very hot tap water
1/4 cup extra virgin olive oil
1 medium onion, halved lengthwise, cut into long thin slices
1 clove garlic, bruised with side of knife
1 2 x 1/2-inch strip orange zest
1 sprig fresh basil (optional)
1 cup dry white wine or chicken broth
2 14 1/2-ounce cans peeled Italian plum tomatoes with juice
8-12 mussels (debearded) and/or clams, scrubbed and refrigerated
4 jumbo or 12 medium shrimp, peeled and deveined, or equivalent
*   amount of scallops*
1 12-ounce firm white fish (cod, halibut, shark) steak cut into
*   1-inch chunks*
Crostini

If including saffron, put threads in small bowl with 1/4 cup very hot water and cover until ready to use.

In large saucepan or deep skillet with tight-fitting lid, heat olive oil over low heat; add onion and garlic and sauté, stirring occasionally, over medium-low heat until onion is tender (about 5 minutes). Add zest, basil, wine or broth and bring quickly to hard boil; boil 1 minute. Add tomatoes and juice and heat to boiling, stirring and breaking up tomatoes with side of spoon. Add saffron threads and soaking liquid. Simmer uncovered 10 minutes.

Add mussels and/or clams, shrimp and fish chunks. Cover and cook over medium-high heat until mussels and/or clams are opened and other fish is cooked through (3-5 minutes).

Crostini: Place 4 1/2-inch-thick slices of Italian or French bread on baking sheet and bake at 350° until dry and lightly toasted on top (15-20 minutes). Rub surface lightly with cut side of garlic clove.

To serve, place one piece of crostini in each of four shallow soup bowls. Add seafood and broth, dividing evenly.

GARLIC SOUP

Serves 5 to 6

6 to 7 tablespoons olive oil
20 cloves garlic, peeled and chopped
6 cups chicken stock - warm
Salt and pepper to taste
Mace to taste
Nutmeg to taste
3 to 4 egg yolks
6 slices french bread, toasted

Garnish: Chopped parsley

In deep pot, sauté garlic gently in 3 tablespoons olive oil, over low heat. Do not brown. Pour in warmed chicken stock; season with salt, pepper, mace and nutmeg. Continue cooking over low heat until garlic is very soft. Place sieve over a pot; pour soup through sieve and return to original pot.

Beat egg yolks with remaining olive oil. Stir some of soup into egg mixture and gradually pour all egg mixture into soup. Do not boil.

Place 1 slice of toasted bread into soup bowl and ladle soup over. Garnish with some chopped parsley and serve immediately.

GAZPACHO

Serves 5
♥

28 ounces fresh tomatoes, chopped
1/4 cup tomato soup concentrate
2 cucumbers, peeled and chopped
2 green peppers, seeded and chopped
1 large clove garlic, chopped
1/2 cup plain bread crumbs
3 to 4 tablespoons red wine vinegar
2 tablespoons ketchup
1/2 teaspoon salt
Pepper to taste
5 tablespoons olive oil
3/4 cup water, or more

Garnish: Chopped tomatoes, red onion, green peppers
*   Crumbled hard-boiled egg (optional)*
*   Fried croutons (optional)*
*   Olive oil*

Mix tomatoes, tomato soup, cucumbers, green peppers, garlic, bread crumbs, vinegar, ketchup, salt, pepper and olive oil in bowl. Purée in food processor or blender, adding water to thin out. Taste for seasoning. Chill for 2 hours or more in refrigerator.

To serve: Ladle into bowls. If too thick, add more water. (May add 1-2 ice cubes, if desired.) Pass garnishes in individual bowls separately.

SOUPS

GREEN PEPPER SOUP

Serves 4 to 5

4 green bell peppers
2 chicken bouillon cubes
1 tablespoon grated white onion
1 tablespoon all-purpose flour
Pinch of cayenne or red pepper flakes, optional
1/4 cup heavy cream

Garnish: 1/2 cup cubed cream cheese

Boil the peppers in 3 cups of water for 10 minutes. Drain (but reserve liquid); put in a plastic bag for 20 minutes. Peel skin; remove seeds and inside ridges.

Make the bouillon with the reserved liquid. Purée the green peppers with 1 cup of water in a food processor or blender.

In a saucepan, melt the butter and sauté the onion until transparent. Add flour and combine with a little remaining broth until smooth. Cook for 1 minute, then add the green peppers. Cook for 5 minutes; add remaining broth, and cayenne to taste. Just before serving, reheat and add the cream. Stir until combined.

To serve, pour hot soup over the cream cheese cubes in individual soup bowls. Serve piping hot.

MINESTRONE

Serves 6

Serve in large soup bowls with portions of pasta and beans in each serving. Top with grated Parmesan cheese. With a green salad and good bread, it makes a hearty winter meal.

3 tablespoons olive oil
1 medium onion, chopped
2 to 3 cloves garlic, crushed
1 tablespoon oregano
1 teaspoon basil
2 cups crushed tomatoes
3 stalks celery, diced
2 medium carrots, sliced
2 medium zucchini, quartered lengthwise and sliced
1 medium turnip, cut into small cubes
1/4 of a small head cabbage, cut into small pieces
1 medium potato, diced
1 quart water
1/2 cup dry red wine
Salt and black pepper to taste
1 cup macaroni (or other small pasta)
1/2 cup cooked chick peas (garbanzos) or other white beans,
        or one 15 ounce can, drained and rinsed
Grated Parmesan cheese

Heat oil in large soup pot and add onions and garlic. Cook until soft but not browned. Add oregano and basil and stir. Add all vegetables except chick peas and add water. Heat to simmer, and cook for 25 minutes or until vegetables are tender. Add salt, pepper and wine to taste.

Cook pasta in boiling water until tender; drain. Combine pasta and chick peas with soup and heat. Sprinkle with Parmesan cheese and serve.

POTATO AND TOMATO SOUP

Serves 4 to 6

1/2 cup water
2 tablespoons (1/4 stick) butter
1 large onion, chopped
1 tablespoon chopped fresh thyme or 1 teaspoon dried, crumbled
1 bay leaf
5 cups chicken broth
3 chicken bouillon cubes
Freshly ground pepper
1 1/2 pounds red new potatoes, peeled and chopped
1 28-ounce can crushed tomatoes with added purée
1/3 cup chopped fresh basil (optional)

Heat water and butter in heavy large saucepan over medium heat. Add onion, thyme and bay leaf. Cover and simmer 5 minutes. Add broth and bouillon cubes. Increase heat and bring to boil.

Reduce heat to medium. Season with pepper. Stir in potatoes and cook until tender, about 10 minutes. Mix in tomatoes with purée and cook until completely heated through. Ladle soup into bowls. Sprinkle with basil, if desired.

ROASTED RED PEPPER SOUP

Serves 6

This soup can also be served cold.

2 pounds red peppers
5 1/2 cups chicken stock
1/2 pound potatoes, peeled, chopped
1/2 medium onion, peeled, chopped
Salt and pepper to taste
1/2 cup fresh cream

Garnish: Chervil sprigs
Swirl of cream

Roast peppers then seed, devein, skin and chop. Boil peppers, potatoes and onion in chicken stock for 10 minutes. Using blender, purée all ingredients together and return to soup pot. Add cream and taste for seasoning.

Serve in bowls, garnishing with a chervil sprig and swirl of cream, if desired.

STRAWBERRY SOUP

Serves 4

1 quart fresh strawberries
2 tablespoons dry white wine
1/4 cup confectioners' sugar
2 cups plain yogurt

Garnish: Fresh mint leaves

Wash, hull and slice strawberries. Place in blender or food processor and blend thoroughly. Pour mixture through sieve to strain. Return the puree to blender. Add wine, confectioners' sugar and yogurt. Blend until well mixed. Chill. Garnish with fresh mint leaves, if desired.

SOUPS

SPLIT PEA SOUP

Serves 4 to 6

1 small ham hock
1 onion, peeled and stuck with 2 cloves
2 stalks celery, halved
1 bay leaf
2 carrots, peeled and halved
1 can (10 ounces) beef broth or bouillon
11/2 cups quick-cooking dried green split peas (if not available,
*   cover dried peas with water and soak overnight)*
Water
Pepper to taste
1/2 cup heavy cream

Place ham, onion, celery, bay leaf, carrots, beef broth and drained split peas in large soup pot. Add water to cover and bring to a boil. Lower heat and simmer covered, stirring occasionally until peas are dissolved, at least one hour.

When done, remove ham and vegetables. Remove cloves from onion and discard.

Place ham, vegetables and onion in processor or blender and process (if desired, ham can be cut into slivers rather than puréed and then added to soup). Return ham mixture to soup and taste for seasoning. Just before serving, add cream and heat gently.

BEEF & PEANUT SALAD (THAI STYLE)

Serves 4 to 6

1 large lettuce (not iceberg), washed, dried and cut into thin strips
1 to 2 Japanese unwaxed cucumbers, semi-peeled and cut into
*   thin rounds*
1 medium red onion, peeled and cut into thin rounds
1 medium carrot, peeled and cut into thin strips
1 bunch radishes (optional), stemmed and cut into thin rounds
1/3 cup green beans or snow peas, stemmed, parboiled, and cooled
3 small hot green chili peppers, minced
1 large knob of fresh ginger, peeled and shredded
2 to 3 large garlic cloves, peeled and minced
Juice of 2 limes
3 to 4 tablespoons safflower or corn oil plus extra to sauté beef
2 tablespoons creamy peanut butter or to taste
1/2 to 1 tablespoon sugar
1 tablespoon or to taste nuoc mam (fish sauce) or soy sauce
Water to thin out dressing
Salt and pepper to taste
1 pound beef, cut into thin strips

Garnish: Chopped fresh cilantro leaves and stems (1 to 2 bunches)
*   1/2 cup dry roasted peanuts, chopped*

Prepare all vegetables and place on either a large serving platter or in large bowl. (Make mounds of individual vegetables on bed of lettuce.)

Make dressing in either a food processor or blender. Blend together the chili peppers, ginger and garlic. Add lime juice, 2 tablespoons oil, peanut butter, sugar and nuoc mam. If too thick, thin out with water. Season to taste with salt and pepper.

Lightly sauté the beef strips in 1 or 2 tablespoons of oil, seasoning to taste with salt and pepper. You may add beef to the salad either hot or cold. Place in center of the salad.

To serve, pour dressing over the salad and generously scatter the cilantro over the top. Sprinkle chopped peanuts over the whole dish. Serve immediately.

SALADS

CHICKEN SALAD

Serves 4

3 pounds chicken breasts, boneless and skinless
6 ounces sherry or wine
2 to 3 tablespoons mayonnaise
1 teaspoon salt
1/4 teaspoon pepper
1/4 teaspoon thyme
1/4 teaspoon nutmeg
6 ounces golden raisins
2 to 3 ounces walnuts, chopped
2 to 3 celery stalks, chopped
2 apples, cored and chopped

Boil chicken in lightly salted water for about 30 minutes. In covered dish, marinate chicken in sherry overnight in refrigerator. Drain off liquid and cut chicken into 1 inch cubes. Coat with mayonnaise; add seasonings. Toss with remaining ingredients, adding apples just prior to serving.

BLACK BEAN SALAD

Serves 8

♥

Dressing
1 cup olive oil
3 tablespoons unseasoned rice vinegar
3 tablespoons balsamic vinegar
1 clove garlic, peeled and minced
1/2 teaspoon sugar (optional)
1/4 teaspoon pepper

Salad
2 cans (16 ounces each) black beans, rinsed and drained
1 package (10 ounces) frozen corn, thawed
2 medium-size red bell peppers, seeded and diced
4 celery stalks, diced
1/2 small onion, finely chopped

Mix all dressing ingredients in a salad bowl. Add vegetables and toss to mix and coat.

CHICKEN AND VEGETABLE SALAD

Serves 8 to 10

1/2 chicken breast, boned and skinned
4 medium carrots, cut in small pieces
1 medium parsnip
3 medium red potatoes, washed
4 dill pickles, cut in pieces
1/4 cup Dijon mustard
1 teaspoon salt
1 cup mayonnaise
1 (4 ounce) can green peas, drained

Garnish: Pitted black olives

Poach chicken, carrots and parsnip in simmering water until tender. Drain and cool. In a separate pot, boil unskinned potatoes and let cool. Remove skin.

Dice the chicken, carrots, parnsip, potatoes and pickles. Mix mustard, salt and mayonnaise in a large bowl. Add the diced chicken, vegetables and peas. Mix well.

Arrange on serving dish, decorating with mayonnaise and black olives. Serve chilled.

CHICKEN-VEGETABLE SALAD WITH HERBED CHEESE DRESSING

Serves 4 to 6

Dressing can be prepared 1 day ahead. Cover and refrigerate. Stir dressing before using.

Dressing
1 package (5 ounces) garlic and herb semisoft cheese at room temperature
1/2 cup plain yogurt
2 teaspoons dried dillweed, or 1 1/2 tablespoons snipped fresh dill
Salt and freshly ground pepper

Salad
2 cups broccoli florets
4 cups diced cooked chicken
3 cups peeled, seeded and diced cucumber
4 to 6 lettuce leaves

Dressing: Purée first 3 ingredients in blender or food processor until smooth. Season with salt and pepper.

Salad: Cook broccoli in large saucepan of boiling water until just crisp-tender, about 3 minutes. Drain, rinse completely. Combine broccoli, chicken, and cucumber in large bowl. Add dressing and toss to coat. Line plates with lettuce. Spoon salad onto lettuce.

54

THAI-STYLE CHICKEN SALAD

Serves 4

Salad
3 whole chicken breasts, skinned, boned and halved
4 cups mixed salad greens, washed and torn into bite-size pieces
2 tablespoons olive oil
1 cup slivered cucumbers
2 small sweet red peppers, thinly sliced (optional)
1/2 medium red onion, thinly sliced
4 tablespoons chopped mint
4 tablespoons chopped basil
1/2 papaya or 1 small mango, peeled, seeded and cubed
4 tablespoons chopped roasted peanuts (optional)
1 lime, cut into wedges

Dressing
4 small shallots or pearl onions, minced
4 cloves garlic, minced
1/2 cup vegetable oil
5 tablespoons lime juice
1/4 cup creamy peanut butter
2 tablespoons soy sauce
1 to 2 tablespoons honey
1 teaspoon or more chili sauce

Grill chicken until done. Cool and shred. Set aside. Prepare salad ingredients.

Sauté shallots and garlic in oil. Cook until the garlic is white - don't allow it to turn brown. Immediately transfer to a blender or food processor with remaining dressing ingredients. Blend thoroughly. Taste for seasoning.

Toss lettuce with olive oil and place on serving plates. Top with chicken, vegetables and fruit. Sprinkle herbs and peanuts on top. Place lime wedge on the side. Spoon some dressing over the salad and pass the rest separately. Squeeze lime juice over the salad, if desired.

CHINESE NOODLE AND CRAB SALAD

Serves 4 to 6

Dressing can be prepared 1 day ahead and refrigerated. Shake before using. Salad can be prepared 2 hours ahead.

Dressing
1/4 cup vegetable oil
1/4 cup fresh lemon juice
1/4 cup chopped fresh cilantro
Salt and freshly ground pepper

Salad
2 cups snow peas, strings removed
1 cup sliced carrots
1 pound chow mein noodles
8 ounces fresh crabmeat, cooked and flaked
1 cucumber, peeled, seeded and diced
1/3 cup chopped scallions (green onions)

Combine first 3 ingredients in a jar with tight-fitting lid. Season with salt and pepper. Seal and shake until well combined.

Cook snow peas and carrots in large saucepan of boiling water until crisp-tender, 1 to 2 minutes. Add noodles and cook until just tender but still firm (al dente), about 1 minute. Drain in a colander and rinse under cold water. Drain completely. Transfer to serving bowl.

Stir in crab, cucumber and scallions. Add dressing and toss to coat. Refrigerate until completely chilled, at least 30 minutes.

FENNEL, ARUGULA & ONION SALAD WITH ORANGES

Serves 6

1 cup fresh orange juice
2 tablespoons white wine vinegar
1 large shallot, sliced
1 bay leaf
1 tablespoon extra-virgin olive oil
Salt and pepper to taste
3 oranges
1 large fennel bulb, trimmed and sliced
2 1/2-ounce package arugula, leaves only
1/2 medium red onion, very thinly sliced

Boil together orange juice, vinegar, shallot and bay leaf until reduced by half. Discard bay leaf, purée mixture in blender. Pour into a bowl and whisk in the oil. Season with salt and pepper and chill.

Cut and peel white pith from oranges. Cut between membranes to release the segments. Toss the fennel, onion and arugula with the dressing. Put in the center of the salad plates and arrange with orange slices around the edge.

GREEN BEANS IN BACON-WALNUT DRESSING

Serves 6 to 8

4 slices bacon
1/4 cup plus 4 tablespoons olive oil
1/4 cup or more red wine vinegar
1 garlic clove, peeled and minced
Salt and pepper to taste
1/2 cup walnuts (or pecans), chopped and toasted
21 ounces green beans, cleaned, stemmed and cut on the diagonal

Garnish: 1 small red onion, cut into paper thin slices and halved

Cook bacon until crisp. Drain bacon on paper towels (but leave at least 2 tablespoons of bacon fat in the pan). Break into small pieces and place into a small mixing bowl.

Add olive oil, red wine vinegar and garlic to the bacon fat in the pan. Turn heat on to medium-high. Season to taste with salt and pepper and boil for one or two minutes. Pour over bacon. Mix in nuts and let stand at least 30 minutes.

Cook beans in salted water until crisp-tender. Drain and plunge into cold water. Place beans in serving dish and toss with dressing. Garnish with red onion and serve.

SICILIAN EGGPLANT SALAD

Serves 6

Can be prepared 2 days ahead and refrigerated.

6 tablespoons olive oil
3 large onions, diced
2 celery stalks, diced
1 1/4 pounds eggplant (about 2 small), cut into 1/2-inch pieces
5 Italian plum tomatoes, peeled, seeded and quartered
1 cup small green olives with pimientos
1/2 cup drained capers
1/2 cup cider vinegar
1/3 cup sugar

Heat 3 tablespoons olive oil in a heavy large skillet over medium heat. Add onions and celery and cook until translucent, stirring often, about 10 minutes. Transfer to heavy large saucepan.

Heat remaining 3 tablespoons oil in same skillet. Add eggplant and cook until golden brown, stirring frequently, about 10 minutes. Add to onion mixture. Add remaining ingredients to onion mixture and bring to a boil, stirring constantly. Reduce heat and simmer until vegetables are soft, stirring occasionally, about 20 minutes.

May be served hot, cold or at room temperature.

SALADS

GREEN SALAD WITH MANGO/CITRUS VINAIGRETTE DRESSING

Serves 4 - 6
♥

Dressing can be used with any salad of your choice.

Dressing
3 tablespoons fresh orange juice
2 tablespoons red wine vinegar
1/2 lemon, juice only
5 tablespoons olive oil
Salt and pepper to taste

Salad
1 ripe medium mango, peeled and diced
2 heads butter lettuce, cleaned and torn into bite-size pieces
1/2 small red onion, sliced paper thin
3 tablespoons toasted and chopped walnuts

Garnish: Minced parsley

Combine dressing ingredients and blend well. Season to taste with salt and pepper.

Place lettuce in a salad bowl, top with the mango, red onion and walnuts. Pour dressing over and top with the parsley. Serve cold.

LINGUINE SALAD WITH SESAME DRESSING

Serves 10

Condiment candidates for this salad would be sliced Chinese sausage, hot chili and/or sesame oil, green onions, toasted sesame seeds, blanched carrot matchsticks, cubed tofu, water chestnuts or peeled jicama and soy sauce.

1 1/2 pounds linguine
1/2 cup sesame oil
1/2 cup light soy sauce
1 tablespoon hot chili oil* (or to taste)
2 teaspoons minced garlic
Salt and freshly ground pepper
1 cup minced arugula, cilantro or watercress
1 orange slice, twisted

Cook linguine in large pot of rapidly boiling salted water until just tender but still firm to bite, stirring to prevent sticking. Drain. Transfer to large bowl.

Combine sesame oil, soy sauce, chili oil and garlic in small bowl and whisk to blend. Season with salt and pepper. Add just enough oil mixture to linguine to coat. Cover and refrigerate linguine at least 3 and up to 8 hours.

Just before serving, add arugula to linguine and toss. Transfer to serving bowl. Top with orange slice. Pour remaining sesame dressing into small bowl and serve with salad.

*Hot chili oil is available at Oriental markets and some supermarkets.

61

POTATO SALAD WITH TARRAGON & ORANGE DRESSING

Serves 6

♥

This potato salad contains no egg or milk products.

6 cups cubed new potatoes
8 green onions (scallions), sliced diagonally
3 tablespoons vegetable oil
1 1/2 tablespoons cider vinegar
1 tablespoon minced fresh tarragon or 1 teaspoon dried
1/2 teaspoon freshly grated orange rind
Dash of ground nutmeg (optional)

Garnish: Tarragon sprigs

Cook potatoes in boiling water until firm-tender, about 10-15 minutes. Add scallions to potatoes and water, turn off heat, cover pan and let sit for about 1 minute.

Whisk oil, vinegar, tarragon and orange rind in large salad bowl. Drain potatoes and scallions; add to dressing in bowl.

Dust with nutmeg, if desired, and toss until potatoes are coated with dressing. Serve the salad either warm or chilled. Garnish with tarragon sprigs.

TUNA, PASTA, BROCCOLI AND RED PEPPER SALAD

Serves 4
♥

Dressing
1/2 cup olive oil
2 tablespoons red wine vinegar
2 tablespoons drained capers
1 teaspoon crumbled, dried oregano
3/4 teaspoon salt
1/2 teaspoon finely minced garlic
1/4 teaspoon freshly ground pepper

Salad
1 bunch broccoli
1/2 pound freshly cooked farfalle noodles or shell macaroni
3 to 4 red bell peppers, cut into 1-inch pieces
*2 cans (6*1/2 *ounces each) solid white tuna, drained and*
coarsely chunked

Combine all dressing ingredients in jar with tight-fitting lid, shake well and refrigerate.

Peel broccoli stems and cut diagonally 1/2 inch thick. Divide florets into 1 inch pieces. Steam stems and florets separately in batches until crisp-tender. Transfer to colander and run under cold water until cooled completely. Pat dry with paper towels. Keep stems and florets separated. Transfer florets to bowl and toss with about 1/4 of dressing.

Combine pasta, peppers and broccoli stems in large serving bowl and toss lightly with remaining dressing. Add tuna and toss gently. Make border of florets around salad. Cover and chill before serving.

SALADS

SHRIMP AND CELERY SALAD WITH WARM DILL DRESSING

Serves 6

4 quarts water
1 tablespoon salt
36 medium shrimp (about 1 1/2 pounds), shelled and deveined
6 celery stalks, cut diagonally into 1-inch pieces
3 tablespoons white wine vinegar
2 tablespoons Dijon mustard
1 teaspoon sugar
Pinch of salt
1/3 cup heavy cream
1/4 cup minced fresh dill
1/3 cup vegetable oil
1 head Bibb or Boston lettuce
1 medium red onion, sliced into thin rings
Freshly ground black pepper (optional)

Bring water and salt to boil in large pot. Add shrimp and celery and cook 1 minute. Drain immediately. Cool to room temperature.

Blend vinegar, mustard, sugar and pinch of salt in heavy small non-aluminum saucepan. Whisk in cream. Place over medium heat and bring just to a simmer, stirring constantly. Stir in dill. Remove from heat. Whisk in oil in thin stream. Cover and do not refrigerate.

Line salad plates with lettuce leaves. Divide shrimp and celery among plates. Garnish with onion. Rewhisk dressing. Spoon over salads. Sprinkle with pepper, if desired.

64

SPICY SHRIMP WITH ORANGES & MINT

Serves 2
♥

Fish sauce is available in Oriental markets and some supermarkets. If you can't find it, substitute about half as much soy sauce.

1 pound large shrimp
5 medium-size oranges, peeled
3 tablespoons freshly-squeezed orange juice
3 tablespoons freshly-squeezed lime juice
2 teaspoons fish sauce
3 or 4 cloves garlic, minced or pressed
1/2 teaspoon minced fresh red chili pepper or dried chili flakes
*   (more or less according to taste)*
Salt to taste

Garnish: 1 cup fresh small whole mint leaves, or 1/2 cup chopped
*   fresh mint leaves*

Boil the shrimp approximately 3 minutes. Cook, then shell and devein, leaving tails on, if desired.

With a small sharp knife, remove all white pith from oranges and cut into segments between the membranes, discarding any seeds.

In a bowl, combine the orange juice, lime juice, fish sauce, garlic, chili pepper, and salt to taste. Add the shrimp and oranges and toss well. Cover and chill for at least 1 hour or up to 4 hours.

Just before serving garnish with mint leaves.

SPINACH SALAD WITH TOASTED ALMONDS & MANDARIN ORANGES

Serves 5

♥

11/2 bunches of spinach, washed and roughly torn apart into bite-size pieces (include the upper stem)
8 tablespoons roasted unsalted almonds, roughly chopped
1 large can mandarin oranges (drained)
Red or white onion, cut into thin rings

Dressing
9 tablespoons olive oil
3 tablespoons raspberry vinegar
3 tablespoons wine vinegar
1/2 teaspoon coarsely-cracked black pepper
3 tablespoons parsley, finely chopped
1/4 teaspoon salt

Put spinach into large serving bowl. Roast almonds in a pan until golden brown, stirring constantly. Top spinach with mandarin oranges and almonds and scatter onion rings over the top.

Make salad dressing by whisking all ingredients together in a small bowl. Pour salad dressing over salad and serve.

WILTED SPINACH SALAD (KOREAN-STYLE)

Serves 4
♥

1 pound fresh spinach, washed, stems removed
2 tablespoons toasted sesame seeds
2 tablespoons soy sauce
2 tablespoons white vinegar
2 tablespoons sesame oil
1 tablespoon sugar

Place spinach (with water clinging to leaves) in large saucepan. Cover and heat until steaming, about 1 minute. Remove from heat, drain and rinse with cold water. Drain again. Squeeze off excess water and coarsely chop.

Combine sesame seeds, soy sauce, vinegar, oil and sugar. Toss with spinach and serve.

COUNTRY-STYLE GREEK SALAD

Serves 6

Dressing
3 tablespoons olive oil
1 1/2 tablespoons white wine vinegar
1/4 teaspoon salt
Fresh pepper to taste

Salad
2 bunches chicory
4 tomatoes, sliced
2 cucumbers, sliced
1/2 cup feta cheese
3 tablespoons capers

Combine dressing ingredients and chill. Line a large shallow salad bowl with chicory and top with slices of tomato and cucumber. Crumble the feta cheese over all and sprinkle with capers. Pour dressing over salad and serve.

SALADS

WATERCRESS AND CORN SALAD WITH GREEN ONION DRESSING

Serves 4

♥

Salad
3 large bunches watercress, stemmed, washed and roughly
chopped
1/2 cup plus 2 tablespoons whole kernel corn
1/3 cup plus 1 tablespoon red onion, chopped

Dressing
1/2 cup plus 2 tablespoons milk
1/2 cup plus 2 tablespoons minced scallions (green onions)
3 tablespoons white wine vinegar
Salt and pepper to taste

Layer the watercress, corn and red onion in a salad bowl. If time permits, chill in the refrigerator until ready to serve.

Whisk together all dressing ingredients and taste for seasoning. Just before serving, pour dressing over salad.

WINTER FRUIT SALAD

Serves 6

Salad
2 cups fresh pineapple chunks
2 firm bananas, peeled and sliced
1 cup seedless grapes
1 cup sliced oranges
1 cup pitted dates
Salad greens to line bottom of plate

Dressing
1 cup vanilla yogurt
Zest and juice of 1 orange
6 pitted dates
1 teaspoon curry powder (optional)

Salad: Combine pineapple, bananas, grapes, oranges and dates. Arrange fruit on individual lettuce-lined plates.

Dressing: Combine yogurt, 1 teaspoon orange zest, 1/2 cup orange juice, dates and curry powder in blender. Blend until smooth, about 30 seconds. Serve salad with dressing.

DRESSINGS

LEMON-MUSTARD SALAD DRESSING

Makes 1 cup

1 cup olive oil
1/4 teaspoon thinly-grated lemon peel
2 tablespoons lemon juice
1 egg yolk
3 cloves garlic, minced
1/2 teaspoon salt
1/2 teaspoon dry mustard
1/4 teaspoon thyme
1/3 teaspoon ground black pepper

In a blender or food processor, blend all ingredients until smooth. Pour into a jar and refrigerate overnight for best flavor.

RED WINE VINAIGRETTE DRESSING

Serves 6

1 cup dry red wine
7 tablespoons red wine vinegar
3 tablespoons white onion, minced
2 large bay leaves, torn in half
3 tablespoons Dijon mustard
1/3 cup safflower oil
1/3 cup olive oil
2 tablespoons dried parsley
Salt and black pepper to taste

Boil wine, 5 tablespoons vinegar, white onion and bay leaves. Reduce to about 2 tablespoons -- it takes about 8 minutes. Stir occasionally. Place in a bowl and let cool. Whisk in remaining vinegar, oils and seasoning.

Serve with salad of your choice.

BASIC WHITE SAUCE

Makes 1 cup

You can add many things to this sauce to change it: spices, cheeses, vegetables, etc.

2 tablespoons butter
2 tablespoons flour
1 cup milk
Salt and pepper to taste

In a saucepan over medium heat, melt butter, but do not let it brown. Add the flour and stir with a wire whisk. In another saucepan heat the milk until it is almost, but not quite, boiling.

Add the hot milk to the flour mixture. Add salt and pepper to taste. Continue stirring while it comes to a boil, then lower the heat and let sauce simmer for at least 5 minutes before you serve it.

SAUCES

SPANISH BANDERILLA SAUCE

Serves 4

3 cloves garlic, peeled and minced
3 tablespoons fresh parsley, minced
3 tablespoons French cornichon pickle, minced
3 tablespoons olive oil

Place all ingredients except the olive oil in a food processor or blender. With the motor running, add the olive oil and blend until smooth.

Suggestions for serving:

Dab any of the following bite-sized ingredients with a bit of sauce and serve at room temperature: drained and rolled anchovies, cooked slices of chorizo sausage, cooked and peeled shrimp, small cooked potatoes (peeled and sliced), cooked asparagus tips, cured black olives, small hard-boiled eggs (sliced in half), cured ham, solid white meat tuna, marinated pearl onions or mushrooms.

You may use cocktail toothpicks to make mini-kabobs of the above ingredients and place around (or in) a small dish of sauce for easier serving.

ITALIAN TOMATO SAUCE

Approximately 8 cups

1/3 cup olive oil
2 medium green peppers, finely diced
1 large yellow onion, finely diced
6 cloves garlic, or to taste, minced
2 28-ounce cans Italian tomatoes, whole or crushed
2 tablespoons Italian spices*
2 tablespoons oregano
1/2 tablespoon basil
1 teaspoon crushed red pepper, or to taste
Small amounts of salt and sugar may be added, very carefully,
*   to taste*

In a large saucepan or small stockpot (6 quarts is more than adequate), pour in olive oil. Add green pepper, onion and garlic. Sauté on medium heat for about 5 minutes (do not brown). Add tomatoes and spices and simmer for approximately 30 minutes.

Use a potato masher to crush tomatoes (crushed are available in cans and make a thicker sauce than whole tomatoes). Simmer for at least 2 hours.

Batch may be doubled and frozen using plastic storage containers.

*Italian spices is an actual mixture available in most supermarkets.

73

SAUCES

DIJON MUSTARD MARINADE

Makes 1 cup
♥

1/3 to 3/4 cup Dijon mustard
1/4 cup or more honey
2 tablespoons or more coarsely-cracked black pepper
3 tablespoons soy sauce
3 tablespoons dry white wine (optional)
1 tablespoon parsley (optional)

Combine all ingredients. Taste for seasoning. Marinate chicken in refrigerator for at least 30 minutes. (Can marinate up to 12 hours.)

Marinade may be used for chicken, pork or beef.

GARLIC MAYONNAISE (AIOLI)

Makes 1 cup

3 egg yolks, room temperature
3 tablespoons or more lemon juice
3 large cloves garlic, peeled and chopped
1 tablespoon Dijon mustard
1/2 teaspoon salt
1/2 cup vegetable oil
1/3 cup olive oil
Freshly-ground black pepper

Blend yolks, lemon juice, garlic, mustard, and salt in processor or blender. With machine running, add oils in very slow steady stream. Mix until thick; add lots of pepper.

SPINACH PESTO

Serves 4

Serve over hot pasta as a first course. Can be stored in your refrigerator in a jar with a thin layer of oil over the top to seal out air. Can also be frozen.

Fresh spinach, enough to half-fill blender
3 sprigs parsley
1/2 cup freshly grated Parmesan cheese
3 cloves garlic, chopped
1 teaspoon salt or more
1/2 cup pine nuts (Pignoli nuts)
1/4 cup olive oil
1/4 cup hot water

In blender, blend spinach, oil, parsley, cheese, garlic and salt. If the mixture starts clogging your blender, add the hot water. Add 1/2 the pine nuts. Blend until smooth. Fold in remaining nuts. Add salt to taste.

PASTA

DAVID B. FINE

NOTES

CAPELLINI WITH ZESTY CRAB SAUCE

Serves 2
♥

1 tablespoon butter
1/2 cup chopped scallion (green onion)
1 garlic clove, minced
2 medium tomatoes, peeled, seeded and chopped
1/4 cup chicken broth
1/2 pound cooked crabmeat, shredded
1 tablespoon lemon juice
1/2 teaspoon celery salt
Freshly ground pepper to taste
1/4 cup chopped fresh parsley
8 to 10 ounces capellini, freshly cooked

Garnish: Parsley sprigs

Melt butter in large skillet over medium heat. Add scallion and garlic. Stir until scallion is tender, about 3 minutes. Add tomatoes and broth. Increase heat and bring to boil, stirring constantly. Reduce heat and simmer 2 minutes.

Stir in crab, lemon juice, celery salt and pepper. Stir in chopped parsley. Mound pasta on serving platter. Stir in crab mixture. Garnish with parsley sprigs.

PASTA PAVAROTTI

Serves 4

A traveler's delight only one pot.

4 cloves garlic, chopped
1 tube Italian tomato-paste concentrate
4 tablespoons olive oil
Crushed red pepper flakes to taste
Parmesan cheese to taste, freshly grated if possible
1 pound spaghetti or linguine, cooked

Mix all ingredients except pasta in a large bowl. Pour cooked pasta over mixture; toss. Add extra Parmesan cheese and serve.

77

PASTA

LASAGNA FLORENTINE

Serves 12 to 16

1 pound package lasagna noodles
3 large eggs
3 pounds ricotta cheese
1/4 pound Parmesan cheese, freshly grated
1 (10 ounce) package chopped frozen spinach, thawed and drained
10 breakfast link sausages, diced, cooked and drained
3 cloves garlic, minced
1 pound mozzarella cheese, shredded
1 package fresh spinach, well washed and trimmed
1/2 pound mozzarella cheese, sliced thin

Italian Tomato Sauce; see Sauces Section for recipe

Cook noodles according to package directions, do not overcook.

In a large mixing bowl, combine eggs, ricotta, Parmesan, chopped spinach, cooked sausage, garlic and shredded mozzarella. Mix well by hand.

In a roasting pan (9 x 13, at least 3½ inches deep) start layering tomato sauce to just cover the bottom, then noodles (just barely overlapping edges), a single layer of fresh spinach, dollops of ricotta mixture (the mixture does not have to be smoothly layered, cooking takes care of that), more fresh spinach; repeat the previous steps. On the top layer of noodles, spread sauce and cover with slices of mozzarella. Bake 1 hour in preheated 350° oven, covered for 45 minutes. Then remove cover and continue baking. Serve with tomato sauce.

Note: Broken noodles can be used on bottom or middle layers. Two packages of frozen spinach may be mixed with ricotta instead of using fresh spinach. Top layer of cheese should be slightly browned and bubbly; if not, place under broiler briefly.

PASTA WITH GOAT CHEESE

Serves 8 as side dish,
3 as entree

1 pound spiral pasta
4 tablespoons (1/2 stick) butter
6 tablespoons olive oil
7 or 8 ounces goat cheese, crumbled
1 (10 ounce) package frozen chopped spinach, cooked and drained
8 fresh plum tomatoes, chopped
2 garlic cloves, minced (optional)
Black pepper to taste

Cook pasta and drain. Put into large bowl. While pasta is hot, add butter, oil and cheese. Mix until pasta is coated with the cheese. Add spinach, tomatoes, garlic and pepper; mix well. Serve hot.

LINGUINE WITH FRESH TOMATO SAUCE

Serves 4
♥

4 tablespoons olive oil
2 tablespoons minced garlic
3 pounds very ripe tomatoes, coarsely chopped, liquid reserved
1/2 cup coarsely chopped fresh basil
3 tablespoons red wine vinegar
Salt and freshly ground pepper
1 pound linguine
1 tablespoon extra-virgin olive oil
Freshly grated Parmesan cheese

Heat 1 tablespoon oil in small heavy skillet over medium-low heat. Add garlic; cook, stirring for 3 minutes; do not brown. Transfer to large non aluminum bowl. Mix in tomatoes and liquid, remaining 3 tablespoons oil, basil and vinegar. Season with salt and pepper. Let stand 6 hours.

Just before serving, cook linguine in large amount of boiling salted water until just tender but still firm to bite. Drain well; transfer to large bowl. Add olive oil and toss well. Reheat sauce, add to pasta, toss again. Pass Parmesan cheese at the table and sprinkle to individual taste.

PASTA

LINGUINE WITH TOMATOES & SHRIMP

Serves 2

4 tablespoons (1/2 stick) butter
1/4 cup olive oil
1 large onion, chopped
8 garlic cloves, minced
11/4 pounds tomatoes, chopped
Half of a 6-ounce can pitted black olives, drained and halved
20 fresh basil leaves, chopped, or 1 tablespoon dried, crumbled
1 teaspoon dried oregano, crumbled
1/2 teaspoon dried rosemary, crumbled
1/2 teaspoon fennel seeds
Salt and pepper to taste
16 medium shrimp, shelled, deveined and cooked
1/2 cup grated Parmesan cheese
8 ounces linguine, freshly cooked

Melt butter with oil in large heavy skillet over medium heat. Add onion and garlic and cook until soft, stirring, about 8 minutes.

Add tomatoes and next 5 ingredients to skillet. Season with salt and pepper. Cook until tomatoes are soft, about 6 minutes. Add shrimp and stir until heated through. Add 1/4 cup Parmesan. Pour over pasta and toss. Serve immediately, passing remaining 1/4 cup Parmesan separately.

PASTA PUTTANESCA

Serves 4
🕐

2 tablespoons olive oil
1 pound pasta of choice
1/4 cup olive oil
1/2 cup chopped onion
4 large garlic cloves, peeled and chopped
1/2 teaspoon or more crushed red pepper flakes
1 (28 ounce) can Italian whole tomatoes
1/4 cup dry red wine
Black pepper to taste
12 or more large black olives, pitted
7 or more anchovy fillets, drained and chopped
3 tablespoons capers, drained and rinsed
3 tablespoons chopped fresh basil

Garnish: Freshly grated Parmesan cheese

Bring a large pot of salted water to a full boil; add 2 tablespoons olive oil, then pasta. Cook until al dente (cooked through, but still firm and slightly chewy). Drain but do not rinse; keep warm.

Sauté onion, garlic and red pepper flakes in 1/4 cup olive oil until soft. Add tomatoes (chop up tomatoes in pan with back of spoon) and red wine; cook for 10 minutes in a covered pan. Stir occasionally. Add pepper, olives, anchovies, capers and basil; cook until heated.

Toss pasta in pan, then pour into serving bowl. Pass Parmesan cheese separately.

PENNE WITH PEPPERS & CREAM

Serves 2

2 large sweet red bell peppers
1 large clove garlic, minced
2 oil-packed sun-dried tomatoes, well drained and minced
Pinch hot red pepper flakes
2 tablespoons heavy cream
Salt to taste
1/2 pound penne pasta
2 tablespoons freshly grated Parmesan cheese

Char peppers under a broiler or over an open flame. Place charred peppers in a plastic bag and keep it closed for a few minutes, then remove peppers and scrape off all the skin. Core, seed and chop peppers coarsely.

Bring a large pot of water to a boil for the pasta.

Heat a large nonstick skillet, add the peppers, garlic and sun-dried tomatoes and cook over medium heat until peppers are tender, about five minutes.

Stir in the pepper flakes and cream and cook a few minutes, until the cream has thickened slightly. Season to taste with salt and remove from heat.

When the water has boiled, add a generous pinch of salt and the penne. Cook the penne until it is al dente, about eight minutes. Drain well and add to the skillet.

Return the skillet to the heat and cook, stirring for a minute or two, until the ingredients are well combined. Stir in the cheese and serve.

LINGUINE WITH PROSCIUTTO & SUN-DRIED TOMATOES

Serves 4

1/4 pound (1 stick) unsalted butter
1/2 cup olive oil
4 cloves garlic, minced
1/4 pound thinly sliced prosciutto, cut in strips
1/2 cup drained sun-dried tomatoes, cut in strips
1/2 cup minced fresh basil
1/2 cup minced fresh Italian parsley
1 pound linguine, freshly cooked
Freshly grated Parmesan cheese

Melt butter with oil in large heavy skillet over medium-low heat. Add garlic and cook until golden, stirring frequently, 1 to 2 minutes. Stir in prosciutto and cook 2 minutes. Add tomatoes, basil and parsley. Increase heat and bring to gentle boil. Place pasta in large serving bowl. Pour sauce over and toss thoroughly. Sprinkle with Parmesan.

VEGETABLE PASTA

Serves 3 to 4

♥

3 tablespoons olive oil
3 cloves garlic, minced
1/4 cup chopped onion
1 pint cherry tomatoes, halved
2 cups chopped broccoli, cooked until crisp-tender and drained
1 tablespoon chopped fresh basil or 1/2 teaspoon dried, crumbled
1/2 teaspoon crushed red pepper flakes, or to taste
Salt and freshly ground pepper
1/2 pound fettuccine, cooked al dente and drained
Freshly grated Parmesan cheese

Heat oil in very large skillet over medium-high heat. Add garlic and onion and sauté until tender, 5 to 10 minutes. Add tomatoes and cook until softened, about 10 minutes. Blend in broccoli and seasonings. Add fettuccine and toss lightly. Sprinkle lightly with Parmesan and toss again. Pass additional cheese at table if desired.

BAKED PENNE WITH SAUSAGE, ZUCCHINI AND FONTINA

Serves 2 to 4

Add a salad and a loaf of Italian bread and you have a complete meal. Can be prepared 1 day ahead. Cover and refrigerate. Bring to room temperature before baking.

3 medium zucchini, trimmed, halved lengthwise
1 tablespoon olive oil
1/2 pound hot Italian sausage, casings removed
1 medium onion, chopped
Salt and freshly ground black pepper
1 cup whipping cream
1 teaspoon dried oregano, crumbled
1/2 pound Fontina cheese, grated
1/2 pound penne or other tubular pasta

Grease a 21/2 to 3-quart deep casserole. Cut each zucchini half in thirds lengthwise, then crosswise in 11/2-inch-long pieces.

Heat oil in heavy large skillet over medium heat. Add sausage and cook until no longer pink, breaking up with fork. Transfer to bowl using slotted spoon. Add onion to skillet and cook until beginning to soften, stirring occasionally, about 5 minutes. Add zucchini. Season with salt and pepper and sauté until almost tender, about 8 minutes. Return sausage to skillet. Add cream and oregano and bring to a boil. Add half of Fontina cheese to sauce and stir just until melted.

Heat oven to 375°.

Meanwhile, cook pasta in large pot of boiling water until just tender but still firm to bite. Drain well. Return to pot. Add sauce and stir to coat. Taste and adjust seasonings. Transfer to prepared casserole. Top with remaining cheese. Bake until heated through, about 15 minutes. Serve hot.

PASTA WITH SCALLOPS & LEMON MUSTARD BUTTER SAUCE

Serves 2; can be
doubled or tripled

1 cup dry white wine
1/2 teaspoon grated lemon peel
1/2 pound bay scallops
2 teaspoons Dijon mustard
1/4 cup (1/2 stick) well-chilled butter, cut into 4 pieces
Salt and freshly ground pepper to taste
8 ounces uncooked capellini (angel hair) pasta
1 tablespoon butter
1 tablespoon snipped fresh chives

Bring wine and lemon peel to simmer in heavy medium skillet. Add scallops and cook until almost opaque, a few minutes. Transfer scallops to bowl using slotted spoon.

Increase heat and boil until wine is reduced to 1/4 cup, about 6 minutes. Reduce heat to low. Whisk in mustard, then 1/4 cup butter, 1 piece at a time. Add scallops and any juices and heat through. Season with salt and freshly ground pepper.

Meanwhile, cook pasta in large pot of rapidly boiling salted water until just tender but still firm to bite. Drain well. Toss with 1 tablespoon butter. Divide between plates. Spoon scallops over. Sprinkle with chives.

POLENTA WITH ROASTED RED PEPPER SAUCE

Serves 8
♥

Vegetable cooking spray (olive oil flavor, optional)
1/2 cup thinly sliced green onions and tops
1 clove garlic, minced
2 cups chicken broth
3/4 cup yellow cornmeal

Red Pepper Sauce
3 pounds red bell peppers, cut into halves and seeded
2 tablespoons lemon juice
1/4 teaspoon red cayenne pepper

Spray bottom of medium saucepan with cooking spray; heat until hot. Sauté onions and garlic until tender. Stir in chicken broth and heat to boiling. Gradually stir cornmeal into boiling broth; reduce heat and simmer until mixture thickens and broth is absorbed, stirring frequently. Pour mixture into greased 51/2 x 41/2 x 2-inch loaf pan. Cool; refrigerate until chilled and firm, at least 2 hours.

Remove polenta from pan; cut into 16 slices. Spray skillet with cooking spray; heat until hot. Cook polenta over medium heat until browned on both sides. Arrange slices on serving platter; serve with Roasted Red Pepper Sauce.

Sauce: Arrange pepper halves, skin sides up, on jelly roll pan. Bake at 400° until skin turns black, about 25 minutes. Place peppers in cold water for several minutes; drain. Peel skin from peppers and discard. Process peppers in blender or food processor until smooth.

Mix in lemon juice and cayenne pepper. Transfer sauce to saucepan and cook over medium heat until hot. Remove from heat and let stand 2 to 3 minutes.

You may use 3 jars (12 ounces) of cooked red peppers instead of fresh red peppers.

PASTA ORECCHIETTE AL TONNO
(SHORT PASTA WITH TUNA)

Serves 4
♥

2 ounces olive oil
10 to 12 cloves garlic, chopped
Salt and pepper to taste
1 large tomato, chopped
12 to 16 ounces fresh tuna, diced
Parsley, chopped
Basil, chopped
1 pound shell-shaped pasta

In a large skillet, heat olive oil and garlic. Season with salt and pepper to taste. Cook until garlic turns brown. Add the tomato, tuna, parsley and basil to the skillet, and cook sauce about 10 minutes until tuna is medium rare - or desired doneness.

In another pot, boil water and add the pasta. Cook pasta to desired tenderness and drain. Add pasta to skillet with the tuna sauce and mix well. Serve while hot.

SESAME NOODLES

Serves 4

3 tablespoons rice vinegar
2 tablespoons Dijon mustard
4 teaspoons sugar
2 tablespoons soy sauce
1/3 cup sesame oil
1/4 cup vegetable oil
Juice of 1 orange
Salt and pepper to taste
8 ounces thin egg noodles
2 tablespoons roasted sesame seeds

Garnish: scallion slices (green onions), optional

Blend first 4 ingredients. Whisk in sesame oil and vegetable oil until smooth. Add orange and salt and pepper. Leave sesame seeds for later. Chill at least 30 minutes.

Cook noodles in boiling water until done. Drain. Toss with dressing and sesame seeds when ready to serve. Garnish with scallion slices.

SPINACH NOODLE PUDDING

Serves about 20

2 packages (10 ounces each) frozen chopped spinach
1 1/3 sticks butter or margarine
16 ounces broad noodles
1 pound grated Swiss or Jarlsberg cheese
2 teaspoons salt
2 teaspoons dried Italian herb seasoning
1 teaspoon dried oregano
1/4 teaspoon pepper
3/4 cup grated Parmesan cheese

Heat oven to 375°. Butter an 11 x 16-inch jelly roll pan or its equivalent (one 8x12 and one 8x8-inch pan).

Cook spinach according to package directions. Drain and press out liquid. Melt butter. Cook noodles until al dente and drain. Combine spinach, noodles, cheese, butter and seasonings, separating spinach so it is distributed throughout noodles. Fill pan with noodle mixture and top with grated Parmesan. Pudding is quite thin and becomes rather crisp. Bake 30 minutes. Serve hot or warm.

SPINACH PASTA WITH GORGONZOLA SAUCE

Serves 4

The rich flavor of Gorgonzola cheese makes this sauce unique. It can be prepared about an hour before serving and gently reheated.

1/4 pound imported Gorgonzola cheese, crumbled
1/2 cup milk
3 tablespoons butter
1/3 cup heavy cream
1 pound spinach pasta, fettuccine or spaghetti, cooked al dente
1/3 cup freshly grated imported Parmesan cheese

Combine Gorgonzola, milk and butter in large, non-aluminum skillet. Place over low heat and stir until smooth. Add cream and stir until sauce is hot and well blended. Add pasta and Parmesan and toss until pasta is evenly coated.

DESPERADO SPAGHETTI

Serves 4

4 to 6 cloves garlic, peeled and chopped
1/4 cup minced onion
2 chili peppers, chopped
1/3 cup olive oil
1/2 cup chopped bacon
1/4 cup dry white wine
1/2 cup chopped fresh tomatoes
1/2 cup chopped fresh basil
1 teaspoon dried basil
Salt and pepper to taste
1 pound spaghetti, cooked
1/4 cup Parmesan cheese

Quickly sauté garlic, onion and chili peppers in large skillet with olive oil. Add chopped bacon and quickly brown. Add white wine and tomatoes to sauce; continue cooking over medium heat, 2 - 3 minutes. Just before serving, add dried and fresh basil, salt and pepper. Toss with hot spaghetti, Parmesan cheese and serve.

TORTELLINI SALAD PRIMAVERA

Serves 8 to 10

2 pounds fresh or frozen spinach-tortellini or cheese-tortellini,
or use both
1 head broccoli, sliced and broken into florets and tender stems
1 pound carrots, peeled and cut diagonally in 1/4 inch slices
3 leeks, well rinsed, dried and cut into julienne strips
1 large, sweet red pepper, seeded, and sliced julienne style
1 large yellow pepper, seeded, and sliced julienne style
1/2 cup fresh chopped basil
1 egg yolk
2 tablespoons fresh lemon juice
1 tablespoon Dijon mustard
1 tablespoon balsamic vinegar
1 cup vegetable oil
1/2 cup olive oil
1 teaspoon dried thyme
Finely grated zest of 1 orange
Salt and freshly ground black pepper to taste

Cook tortellini in boiling salted water. Drain and place in large bowl.

Cook broccoli, carrots and leeks until crisp tender. Drain and combine with tortellini. Add red and yellow peppers and basil; toss.

Blend egg yolk, lemon juice, mustard and vinegar in food processor or blender. With the machine running, pour in oil in a thin steady stream to make a light mayonnaise. Add the thyme, orange zest, and salt and pepper to taste.

Pour the dressing over the salad, toss and coat thoroughly. Serve at room temperature, or put in a tightly sealed refrigerated container and serve the next day, after the flavors have mixed well.

NOTES

ARROZ CON POLLO (CHICKEN WITH RICE)

Serves 4

3 pounds chicken cut into bite-size pieces
Salt and pepper
2 tablespoons olive oil
1 cup chopped onion
1 chopped red bell pepper
2 cloves garlic, crushed
1 (16 ounce) can whole tomatoes, drained (save juice),
     and chopped coarsely
Water
1 cup rice (long grain, preferably Uncle Ben's) uncooked
1/2 cup dry white wine
1 bay leaf
1 tablespoon lemon juice
1 teaspoon bijol or saffron*
Dash of salt and pepper
1/2 cup cooked green peas

Sprinkle chicken with salt and pepper. Brown chicken in hot oil over medium heat in very large skillet, approximately 5 minutes. Remove chicken from skillet and set aside.

Add onions, pepper, and garlic. Cook over medium heat for 3 minutes. Add water to the reserved tomato juice to make 2 cups. Add tomatoes, juice, rice, wine, bay leaf, lemon juice, bijol and dash of salt and pepper to skillet. Bring to a boil. Then lower heat and add chicken and simmer, covered for approximately 35 minutes. Add peas, stir and serve.

*Bijol is sold in Spanish specialty markets. It is a red powder used for food coloring. If you use saffron -- use very little, it will color, but also has a slight flavor.

CHICKEN-ARTICHOKE-MUSHROOM SAUTÉ

Serves 4

You can substitute veal scallops in place of chicken breasts.

2 large chicken breasts, boned, skinned and halved
Flour for coating chicken
4 tablespoons (1/2 stick) butter
8 to 10 mushrooms, sliced
1 (15-ounce) can artichoke hearts, rinsed and well drained
1/2 cup chicken stock or broth
1/4 cup white wine
Juice of 1/2 lemon or to taste
Salt and freshly ground pepper to taste

Dredge chicken with flour; shake off excess. Heat butter in medium skillet; add chicken and sauté until golden brown and cooked. Transfer to heated platter.

Add mushrooms to skillet and saute 1 to 2 minutes. Stir in artichoke hearts, stock, wine, lemon juice, salt and pepper to taste and let cook until sauce is reduced slightly, stirring occasionally.

Return chicken to skillet and warm through. Serve immediately.

BASIL-ROASTED CHICKEN WITH GARLIC

Serves 6

4 chicken breasts, split (8 halves)
4 tablespoons (1/2 stick) butter, room temperature
4 teaspoons dried basil
1/2 teaspoon salt
1/4 teaspoon black pepper
1 large bunch fresh basil, roughly chopped
15 large cloves garlic, peeled
1/2 cup dry white wine
1 cup chicken stock
1 bunch chopped fresh basil

Garnish: basil sprigs, optional

Heat oven to 400°

Make a pocket between the skin and meat of the chicken. Set aside. Mix the butter, dried basil and salt and pepper together. Place half of the mixture under the chicken skin; rub remaining mixture over the chicken. Salt and pepper to taste. Tuck the roughly chopped basil on top of the butter under the skin. Place in a greased pan, skin side up. Bake for 15 minutes. Add garlic and wine. Turn chicken over and baste. Reduce heat to 350° and bake another 15 minutes. Remove from oven and keep chicken warm.

Transfer garlic, chicken stock, and 4 tablespoons pan juice to food processor and process until smooth. Place into a saucepan and boil until slightly thickened, 3 to 4 minutes. Season to taste with salt and pepper and add the remaining chopped basil. Slice chicken thickly; top with the sauce and sprig of basil, if desired. Serve immediately.

CHICKEN CUTLETS IN TOMATO-WINE SAUCE

Serves 4 to 6

1/2 cup flour
1/2 teaspoon salt
3 chicken breasts, boned and split
1/4 cup oil

Sauce
1 clove garlic, minced
1 (16-ounce) can crushed tomatoes
1/2 cup dry red wine
1/3 cup sliced fresh mushrooms
1 teaspoon dried oregano
Salt and pepper to taste

In a large bowl, mix the flour with the salt. Dip the chicken cutlets in the flour mixture; heat oil in skillet and brown the chicken on both sides. Remove chicken from skillet and keep warm.

In the drippings, sauté the garlic. Add the tomatoes and wine slowly (so not to splatter) and let simmer for 15 minutes. Then add mushrooms, oregano, salt and pepper. Simmer for another 10 minutes. Place the chicken in the sauce and heat over a low flame for 10 more minutes or until chicken is done. Serve over pasta or with rice.

CHICKEN CHILI

Serves 4

6 tablespoons olive oil
1 large onion, peeled and chopped
4 cloves garlic, peeled and minced
2 sweet red bell peppers, seeded, cored and diced
1 small can mild green chilies, minced
3 tablespoons chili powder
11/2 teaspoons cumin seeds
1 teaspoon ground coriander
Pinch ground cinnamon
1 tablespoon or more flour
3 chicken breasts split, skinned, boned and cubed
2 cans tomato purée
2 tablespoons ketchup
1/4 cup or more pitted black olives, sliced
1 (12 ounce) can beer
1 teaspoon unsweetened cocoa
Salt to taste (optional)

Garnish: Tortilla chips, sour cream, grated cheddar cheese,
    chopped onion, diced avocado (optional)

Heat olive oil in deep heavy pot; add onion and garlic. Sauté over high heat
for 5 minutes. Add red peppers and chili peppers; sauté an additional 5 to
10 minutes over medium heat. Stir in chili powder, cumin, coriander and
flour; cook a few minutes until well blended. Remove from heat.

In a large skillet, sauté chicken in remaining olive oil until browned on both
sides. Remove chicken from skillet. Add chicken, tomato purée, ketchup,
olives and beer to vegetable mixture; stir to blend. Simmer, covered over
low heat 20 to 25 minutes. Stir in cocoa and season to taste with salt. If
chili appears too thin, make a paste of 1 tablespoon each flour and water
and add it to chili to thicken. Serve immediately in soup bowls, passing
garnishes separately at table.

CINNAMON CHICKEN

Serves 2 to 4

4 boneless chicken breasts, split
1/4 teaspoon ground cinnamon
1/4 teaspoon ground cloves
Salt and freshly ground pepper
2 tablespoons vegetable oil
3/4 cup chopped onion
2 garlic cloves, minced
3/4 cup fresh orange juice
2 tablespoons raisins
1 tablespoon capers, drained and rinsed

Pat chicken dry. Season with cinnamon, cloves, salt and pepper. Heat oil in heavy large skillet over medium-high heat. Add chicken skin side down and cook until browned, about 3 to 4 minutes. Add onions and garlic. Turn chicken and cook until second side is brown, stirring onions and garlic frequently, about 3 to 4 minutes.

Pour off oil in skillet. Add orange juice, raisins and capers to skillet. Reduce heat to low. Cover and cook until juices run clear when chicken is pierced with sharp knife, about 15 to 20 minutes. Serve immediately.

GOLDEN CURRIED CHICKEN

Serves 8

4 chicken breasts split, skinned and boned
1/4 cup (1/2 stick) butter
1/3 cup honey
1/4 cup Dijon mustard
2 tablespoons prepared mustard
1 small clove garlic, crushed
2 teaspoons fresh lemon juice
2 teaspoons curry powder
1 teaspoon salt
Freshly cooked rice

Heat oven to 350°

Butter a 9 x 13 inch ovenproof glass baking dish. Arrange chicken in prepared dish. Set aside.

Melt butter in medium saucepan over medium heat. Add next 7 ingredients and whisk until smooth. Pour over chicken. Cover with foil and bake 10 minutes. Uncover and baste with sauce. Continue baking, uncovered, basting occasionally, until chicken is opaque and juices run clear when pierced with tip of sharp knife, 15 to 20 minutes. Serve hot over freshly cooked rice.

POULTRY

GRILLED CHICKEN WITH WALNUT SAUCE

Serves 6

<u>Sauce</u>
2 tablespoons butter
1/4 cup minced onion
4 cloves garlic, peeled and minced
Large dashes: ground cloves, cinnamon, cayenne and saffron
1 bay leaf
1 to 2 tablespoons flour
1 1/2 cups chicken stock
Salt and pepper to taste
1 cup ground walnuts

<u>Chicken</u>
4 medium breasts, split (8 halves)
Salt and pepper to taste
Vegetable oil

Garnish: minced fresh parsley (optional)

<u>Sauce</u>: Melt butter in pan over medium heat. Add onion, garlic, cloves, cinnamon, cayenne, saffron and bay leaf; sauté about 3 minutes. Add flour and stir about 2 minutes. Add stock and bring to a boil, whisking constantly. Boil until sauce thickens. Reduce heat to low and season to taste with salt and pepper. Add walnuts and cook an additional 5 minutes. Remove bay leaf.

<u>Chicken</u>: Season chicken breasts to taste with salt and pepper. Brush with vegetable oil and grill or bake at 400° until cooked. Slice thick. Remove skin if desired. Place chicken breasts on individual plates and top with walnut sauce. Sprinkle with parsley, if desired.

CHICKEN BREASTS WITH GARLIC AND BALSAMIC VINEGAR

Serves 6

This dish is nice accompanied by rice and a brightly colored vegetable such as carrots or broccoli.

4 skinless, boneless chicken breasts, split (8 halves)
3/4 pound small to medium-size fresh mushrooms
2 tablespoons flour
Salt and pepper to taste
2 tablespoons olive oil
6 cloves garlic, peeled
1/3 cup balsamic vinegar
3/4 cup fresh or canned chicken broth
1 bay leaf
1/2 teaspoon minced fresh thyme or 1/4 teaspoon dried

Sprinkle chicken with salt and pepper. Scrub the mushrooms and pat dry.

Season flour with salt and pepper and dredge chicken breasts in the mixture. Shake off excess flour.

Heat oil in large heavy skillet over medium-high heat and cook chicken breasts until nicely browned on one side, about 3 minutes. Add garlic cloves. Turn chicken pieces and scatter the mushrooms over them. Continue cooking, shaking the skillet and redistributing the mushrooms so that they cook evenly. Cook about 3 minutes and add the vinegar, broth, bay leaf and thyme.

Cover tightly and cook over medium-low heat for 10 minutes. Turn pieces occasionally as they cook. Transfer chicken to a warm serving platter and cover with foil. Cook the sauce with the mushrooms uncovered, over medium-high heat for about 4 minutes or until reduced by half.

Discard the bay leaf. Pour the mushrooms, and sauce over the chicken and serve. The garlic may be discarded.

QUICKEST JAMBALAYA

Serves 2

1 (28-ounce) can stewed tomatoes
1 1/4 cups sliced pepperoni
1 cup water
1 medium onion, chopped
1 green bell pepper, seeded and chopped
1 teaspoon freshly ground pepper
1/2 teaspoon chili powder
1/2 teaspoon garlic powder
1/4 teaspoon cayenne pepper
1/8 teaspoon hot pepper sauce
1 cup long-grain rice
2 boneless chicken breasts, split, skinned and diced

Combine first 10 ingredients in large heavy saucepan over medium-high heat. Bring to boil, stirring occasionally. Reduce heat and add rice. Cover and simmer 20 minutes, stirring occasionally.

Mix in chicken. Cover and continue simmering until liquid evaporates and chicken is cooked through. Serve immediately.

JERK CHICKEN

Serves 4

Jerking comes from Jamaica and has been used as a method of food preservation for over 300 years. It is possible to "jerk" anything; seafood, beef, etc. The more Jerk Marinade used, the spicier the chicken.

4 chicken breasts, split with skin

Marinade
1/2 tablespoon coriander seeds
1/2 tablespoon cumin seeds
1/2 to 1 teaspoon black peppercorns
1/4 to 1/2 teaspoon crushed red pepper flakes
1 whole clove garlic
2 generous teaspoons minced fresh ginger
1 tablespoon ground all-spice
1/2 teaspoon salt
1 tablespoon rum
*2**1/2** tablespoons ketchup*
2 tablespoons soy sauce
2 tablespoons vegetable oil
Generous dashes of ground cinnamon and nutmeg
1/4 cup fresh parsley, stemmed and minced
3 tablespoons minced scallion (green onion)

Garnish: Lemon wedges

Toast coriander and cumin seeds, black peppercorns, red pepper and garlic in dry pan for 1 to 2 minutes, until you can smell aroma and pan ingredients become lightly browned. Blend together well. Combine with rest of marinade ingredients in food processor or blender. Rub 2 teaspoons Jerk Marinade over each chicken breast. Cover with plastic wrap and refrigerate for 1 hour or more.

Grill, barbecue, or bake at 325° until done. Serve immediately with lemon wedges on side.

CHICKEN WITH MUSTARD AND TARRAGON

Serves 6

2 tablespoons butter
2 tablespoons olive oil
4 large chicken breasts, skinned, boned and quartered
1/4 cup minced onion
1/4 cup dry white wine
1 cup chicken stock
2 cloves garlic, peeled, minced
1/2 cup heavy cream
4 tablespoons Dijon mustard
1 tablespoon chopped fresh tarragon, or 1 teaspoon dried
1 teaspoon chopped fresh thyme, or 1/2 teaspoon dried
Pinch fresh ground pepper

Garnish: 3 tablespoons parsley
   Freshly cooked rice

In a large pan, heat 1 tablespoon butter and 1 tablespoon oil. Add chicken and sauté until browned on both sides. Remove from pan and keep warm.

Add rest of butter and oil to pan. Add onion and sauté until lightly browned. Add wine, stock, garlic and bring to a boil. Boil until sauce is reduced and thickened. Whip in cream and mustard. Add tarragon, thyme, pepper and taste for seasoning.

Add chicken to sauce and reheat gently. Serve over rice garnished with parsley if desired.

CHICKEN AND PASTA

Serves 3

2 chicken breasts, boned and halved
3 cups undrained canned whole tomatoes
1 green bell pepper, chopped
1/2 medium onion, chopped
1 tablespoon lemon juice
1 teaspoon dried oregano
1 teaspoon salt, optional
1/4 teaspoon black pepper
2 cups sliced green beans
10 pitted black olives, sliced
1 pound small pasta, cooked
Grated Parmesan cheese
Warm Italian bread

Put the chicken, tomatoes, green pepper, onion, lemon juice, oregano, salt and pepper in a Dutch oven or deep skillet. Cover and simmer for 20 minutes. Add the green beans and simmer for 15 minutes, then add the olives and the cooked pasta. Stir thoroughly and serve with Parmesan cheese and warm Italian bread on the side.

CHICKEN STEW WITH MUSHROOMS AND POTATOES

Serves 4

6 tablespoons olive oil
1 chicken, about 3 1/2 pounds, cut into serving pieces
1/4 cup flour
1 small onion, finely chopped
2 or 3 cloves garlic, finely minced
1 pound small red boiling potatoes, cut into bite-size pieces
1 cup chicken or beef broth
1 cup red wine
2 or 3 bay leaves
2 or 3 branches fresh thyme
1 pound tomatoes (fresh or canned), peeled (if fresh), seeded and chopped
1 pound fresh mushrooms, thickly sliced
Salt, freshly ground pepper to taste
1/4 cup chopped parsley (optional)
1 tablespoon chopped fresh thyme (optional)

Heat 2 tablespoons of the oil in a sauté pan or deep skillet. Dredge the chicken in flour. Shake off the excess, and add the chicken to the pan. Brown the chicken on all sides over moderate heat. Remove the chicken from the pan.

Add the onion and garlic to the pan. Cook until they soften, then stir in 1 tablespoon of the flour left from dredging the chicken. Add the potatoes, broth, wine, bay leaves, thyme and tomatoes. Return chicken to the pan, cover pan and let simmer for 20 minutes.

In a separate large skillet, heat the remaining 4 tablespoons of olive oil and sauté the mushrooms in the oil until they are quite brown, about 10 minutes. Season them with salt and pepper as they cook.

After the chicken has simmered for 20 minutes, uncover the pan and add the mushrooms. Let the stew cook gently until the chicken is done, 10 to 20 minutes longer. Remove the chicken, and if the potatoes are not completely soft, let them simmer until done.

Sprinkle with chopped parsley mixed with chopped thyme, if desired.

SOUTH-OF-THE-BORDER STEW

Serves 7 - 8

This stew tastes better the second day.

11/2 *pounds chicken parts with bone*
4 *cups chicken stock*
1 *chicken bouillon cube*
1/2 *beef bouillon cube*
1 *cup dry white wine*
1 *medium onion, peeled and sliced*
5 *cloves garlic, peeled and sliced*
3 *tomatoes, sliced*
1/2 *Jalapeño pepper, seeded and cut up*
11/2 *small cans drained mild green chili peppers, cut into strips*
5 *medium carrots, peeled and sliced into rounds*
2 *medium potatoes, peeled and sliced*
1 *(8 ounce) can corn kernels, drained*
8 *ounces pumpkin, peeled and sliced*
Salt and pepper to taste

Garnish: warm tortillas (optional)

To large soup pot, add chicken, stock, bouillon cubes, 1/2 cup wine, onion and garlic. Bring to a boil, then simmer for 20 minutes. Remove chicken, debone and cut into slices.

Return chicken to soup and add rest of wine plus all other ingredients. Bring to a boil again, cover, reduce heat and simmer another 20 minutes. Test vegetables for doneness and taste for seasoning. Serve hot, with warm tortillas, if desired.

WINE-POACHED CHICKEN BREASTS WITH MUSTARD SAUCE

Serves 4 to 6

♥

6 skinned and boned chicken breast halves
3/4 cup dry white wine
1 1/2 cups chicken broth
1 teaspoon dried tarragon
4 teaspoons Dijon mustard (more, if desired)
2 tablespoons drained and rinsed capers (more, if desired)
4 tablespoons (1/2 stick) butter
3 tablespoons flour
Salt and pepper to taste

Garnish: 3 tablespoons unsalted shelled pistachio nuts,
    coarsely chopped

Place chicken in a single layer in a large frying pan. Add wine, chicken broth, tarragon, mustard and capers. Cover and gently simmer for 15 minutes, or until cooked through. Remove from pan and keep warm.

Mix butter and flour and drop into the poaching liquid to thicken. Whisk over medium-high heat until blended, and cook for 5 minutes. Season to taste with salt and pepper.

Spoon the sauce over the chicken and, if desired, sprinkle with the pistachio nuts.

CORNISH HENS WITH HERB BUTTER

Serves 4

Herb Butter
4 tablespoons (1/2 stick) unsalted butter, softened
2 tablespoons assorted fresh herbs, minced
1 teaspoon brandy
Salt and pepper (optional)

Hens
2 large Cornish hens, halved, washed, dried with paper towels
1 lemon
Vegetable oil
Salt and pepper to taste
Assorted dried herbs (parsley, tarragon, rosemary, basil, thyme)

Garnish: Lemon slices

Combine softened butter, fresh herbs and brandy. Add a little salt and pepper, if desired. Place on waxed paper and roll into a thick log. Place in freezer for at least 45 minutes.

Heat oven to 375°.

Rub hens with lemon juice and oil. Season to taste with salt and pepper. Sprinkle with dried herbs. Place in large greased baking pan. Bake for 1 hour, skin should be golden brown.

To serve: Place one serving of cornish hen on each plate and top with thick slice of herb butter. A slice of lemon may also be used as garnish. Serve immediately.

DUCK IN SOY-GRAND MARNIER SAUCE

Serves 4

Duck
4 to 6 giant (elephant) garlic cloves, peeled and sliced thick
Unsalted butter (approximately 9 tablespoons)
6 ounces shiitake mushrooms, stemmed and halved
6 ounces green beans, cleaned, trimmed and cut into 3-inch pieces
1 pound duck breast

Soy-Grand Marnier Sauce
2 tablespoons butter
1 large orange, zest only cut in strands or slivers, plus juice of
*   1/2 orange*
2 tablespoons low sodium soy sauce
1/4 cup plus 2 tablespoons Grand Marnier, or any orange based
*   liqueur*
1 to 2 tablespoons cold butter

Garnish: watercress leaves or sprigs of Italian parsley

Duck: Sauté garlic in 1 to 2 teaspoons butter until lightly browned. Set aside, cover to keep warm. Do same with mushrooms. Parboil green beans in lightly salted water; drain and lightly sauté in 1 to 2 teaspoons butter. Set aside and also keep warm. Season each vegetable with salt and pepper, as desired.

In another pan, sauté duck in 1 tablespoon butter over medium heat. Cook to desired doneness. Set aside and keep warm.

Sauce: To remaining duck drippings, add 2 tablespoons butter and turn heat back up to medium. Add orange zest, orange juice, soy sauce and Grand Marnier. Cook a few minutes until sauce cooks down, stirring continually. To thicken sauce, just before serving, add 1 to 2 tablespoons cold butter and stir until thoroughly combined.

Place garlic, mushrooms and green beans along edges of platter in a half-circle. Thinly slice the duck and place in center of veggies. Lightly spoon Soy-Grand Marnier sauce over duck. Top with watercress or parsley. Serve immediately.

As an alternative, mushrooms and green beans may be steamed instead of sautéed.

QUAIL IN APPLE BRANDY SAUCE

Serves 8

8 quail, head and feet cut off, wash and pat dry
Salt and pepper to taste
8 sprigs parsley
2 tablespoons melted butter
8 slices blanched bacon

Sauce
1/4 cup apple brandy (Calvados)
1/2 cup dry white wine
3 tablespoons chilled, cubed butter
Salt and pepper to taste

Garnish: watercress or parsley

Heat oven to 400°

Salt and pepper quail to taste. Place sprig of parsley inside cavity. Brush with melted butter and lay bacon slices over quail (use one whole slice per quail). Place in heated oven for 5 minutes, then turn heat down to 350° and continue baking for 15 to 20 minutes until desired doneness. Remove from oven and keep warm.

Sauce: In skillet, add any pan drippings from quail. Flambé* with apple brandy. Add white wine and season to taste. Turn heat up to high and cook until volume is slightly reduced. Then, while stirring, add bits of butter to thicken. Pour sauce over quail and garnish plate with watercress or parsley. Serve immediately.

*Be very careful when you flambé, as the flame can flare up. Use a long match and avert your face.

111

NOTES

BOUILLABAISSE

Serves 6

1 cup chopped white onion
1/2 cup minced leeks (white part only)
1/2 cup olive oil
4 large cloves garlic, peeled and mashed
4 medium tomatoes, roughly chopped
7 cups water
1 teaspoon fish stock granules (Fumet de Poisson)
1/2 bunch fresh parsley sprigs
1/2 teaspoon dried thyme flakes
Pinches of fennel and anise
2 large pinches saffron
1 large strip orange peel
1 bay leaf
1/2 teaspoon salt or to taste
Black pepper to taste
1 tablespoon Pernod or anise liquor
3 pounds assorted white fish and shellfish
6 slices French bread, rubbed with garlic, drizzled with a little
    olive oil and toasted
Fresh parsley, minced

In a deep soup pot, sauté onion and leeks in olive oil over low heat for about 5 minutes or until soft. Add garlic and tomatoes, raise heat and cook an additional 5 minutes, stirring occasionally.

Add water, herbs, seasonings and liquor and bring to a boil. Boil 5 minutes, then add white fish. Boil a few minutes and then add shellfish. Skim off scum. Do not overcook! Fish should remain tender but firm. Total cooking time of fish should not exceed 15 minutes. Taste for seasonings and adjust. More salt might be needed. Remove parsley, orange peel and bay leaf.

To serve: place 1 slice toasted bread in soup bowl; ladle soup over with an assortment of fish. Sprinkle with parsley. Serve immediately. Place a large bowl in center of table for shells and bones.

113

SEAFOOD

GRILLED SHRIMP

Serves 2

🕐

1/3 cup bread crumbs
1/3 cup olive oil
1 garlic clove, minced
1 tablespoon minced fresh parsley
11/2 teaspoons finely chopped fresh basil
Salt and freshly ground pepper
1 pound large or jumbo shrimp (15 or less), peeled and deveined

Heat oven to 425°

Combine first 5 ingredients with salt and pepper to taste. Pat generous amount onto each shrimp. Cover and refrigerate overnight.

Position rack in upper third of oven. Place shrimp on baking sheet and bake, turning once, until shrimp lose translucency and coating is golden brown, about 3 to 4 minutes per side (exact time will depend on size of shrimp).

GREEK-STYLE SHRIMP

Serves 2

2 tablespoons olive oil
1 cup sliced scallion (green onion)
4 cloves garlic, minced
1 pound large shrimp, shelled and deveined
3/4 cup vegetable juice cocktail
1/3 cup crumbled feta cheese
Dash black pepper
2 tablespoons chopped parsley

Heat oil in 10-inch skillet over medium heat. Sauté scallion and garlic in oil until tender. Add shrimp and cook until they turn pink, stirring constantly.

Stir in vegetable juice cocktail. Bring mixture to boil, then reduce heat and simmer, 2 minutes. Sprinkle with cheese and place under broiler. Heat 3 minutes or until cheese is lightly melted. Sprinkle with pepper and parsley.

SHRIMP ITALIANO

Serves 4

This sauce is fantastically rich and delicious.

1 pound medium to large fresh shrimp
1 1/2 sticks butter or margarine
1/4 cup olive oil
1 tablespoon dried parsley
3/4 teaspoon dried basil
1/2 teaspoon dried oregano
2 cloves garlic, minced
1/2 teaspoon salt
1 teaspoon lemon juice

Heat oven to 450°

Peel and devein the shrimp. (To devein, make a shallow cut along the front and back of the shrimp and remove the thin tubes - one dark and one pale- from the shrimp, making sure to leave the tail intact.) Now, make a deeper cut along the inside of each shrimp, almost to the tail, and spread open like a butterfly. Place shrimp side by side in a buttered baking dish.

Melt the butter or margarine in a small saucepan and stir in the remaining ingredients. Pour this evenly over the shrimp. Bake for about 5 minutes in the oven and then place in broiler for an additional 5 minutes.

SEAFOOD

BAKED SCALLOPS

Serves 4

1 pound scallops (if large, cut in half)
1/2 cup butter, softened
2 tablespoons minced shallot
2 tablespoons minced scallion (green onion)
1/2 cup bread crumbs
1 tablespoon lemon juice
1/4 cup chopped walnuts
1/4 teaspoon salt
Freshly ground pepper

Heat oven to 425°

Blend all ingredients together. Place in medium size casserole. Bake for 5 to 6 minutes. Then broil until top is browned. Serve immediately.

BREADED SHRIMP AND SCALLOP KEBABS

Serves 2

1/2 cup bread crumbs
1/2 cup olive oil
1/3 cup chopped parsley
3 garlic cloves, minced
Salt and freshly ground pepper
1 pound uncooked large shrimp, peeled and deveined
1 pound sea scallops

Garnish: Lemon wedges

Combine first 4 ingredients in large bowl. Season with salt and pepper. Pat shrimp and scallops dry. Add to bread crumb mixture and stir until well coated. Cover and refrigerate overnight.

Preheat broiler. Thread shrimp and scallops alternately on metal skewers. Press extra bread crumb mixture onto shellfish. Broil until golden brown, about 3 minutes per side. Serve hot with lemon wedges.

116

SCALLOPS FLORENTINE

Serves 2 to 3

1 pound fresh spinach, or one 10-ounce package frozen spinach,
*   thawed and drained*
1 pound scallops
1 tablespoon finely chopped shallots
4 tablespoons butter
Salt and freshly ground pepper to taste
1/4 cup white wine
2 tablespoons flour
1 cup milk
1/2 cup Gruyère cheese, shredded
1/2 cup heavy cream
1/8 teaspoon grated nutmeg
2 tablespoons grated Parmesan cheese

If the spinach is in bulk, remove and discard any tough stems or blemished leaves. Rinse the spinach and drain well. Cook the spinach briefly until the leaves wilt. Drain well, chop, set aside.

Combine the scallops, shallots, one tablespoon of butter, salt, pepper and wine in a saucepan. Bring just to a boil. Do not cook further. Using a slotted spoon, remove the scallops and set aside. Reserve the cooking liquid.

Melt two tablespoons of butter in a saucepan and add the flour, stirring with a wire whisk. When blended, add the milk and stir rapidly until thickened and smooth. Add the scallop liquid and 1/2 cup shredded Gruyère cheese, and stir. Add the cream and simmer about five minutes, stirring.

Meanwhile, heat the remaining butter in a skillet and add the spinach. Toss briefly just to heat through. Add salt, pepper and nutmeg. Toss. Spoon the mixture into an oval gratin dish and spread it out evenly. Cover with an even layer of scallops. Spoon the sauce over and sprinkle the grated cheese over all.

Place the dish under a preheated broiler and broil to glaze the top. Or bake at 450° for about five minutes.

SCALLOPS IN PESTO SAUCE

Serves 2

Pesto can be frozen in small batches. Can also be served over pasta. This dish can also be an appetizer.

Pesto Sauce (makes 2 cups)
4 cups fresh basil, tightly packed
1/2 cup olive oil
2 cloves garlic, crushed
6 sprigs parsley
Salt and pepper to taste
1/4 cup pine nuts or chopped walnuts
1/2 cup freshly grated Parmesan or romano cheese

Scallops
1 carrot cut julienned
1 clove garlic, crushed
2 tablespoons olive oil
1 chopped scallion (green onion)
1 small tomato, diced
1 pound scallops
3 tablespoons dry white wine
1 tablespoon lemon juice
1 tablespoon Pesto
Salt and pepper to taste

Pesto Sauce: Place all ingredients except cheese in food processor or blender. Blend until all are chopped very fine. Remove from blender or processor and mix with grated cheese.

Scallops: In a large frying pan, heat oil and sauté the carrot and garlic for a minute or two. Add the scallion and tomato. Sauté until the tomato is soft. Keep the heat on high and add the scallops. Sauté just until tender, less than 5 minutes. Add the wine, lemon juice, pesto, salt and pepper. Toss quickly and serve.

VALENCIAN PAELLA

Serves 4

1/4 cup olive oil
3 cloves garlic, peeled and cut in half
1 pound chicken, skinless, boneless and cut into bite-size pieces
1 onion, peeled and chopped
3 medium tomatoes, stemmed and chopped
3 small red bell peppers, seeded and sliced
1 teaspoon paprika
2 cups rice, uncooked
1 teaspoon saffron
4 cups chicken stock
1 cup green peas
3 1/2 ounces chorizo sausage, thickly sliced
16 ounces medium shrimp, shelled and deveined

Garnish: Lemon wedges

In a deep frying pan or wok, heat oil; add garlic and cook until brown. Discard garlic. Brown chicken in garlic-oil; add onion, tomatoes and red pepper. Cook until vegetables are slightly softened. Reduce heat and add paprika. Cook an additional 5 to 10 minutes. Take out all ingredients and set aside.

In same pan, sauté rice in remaining oil. If there is not enough oil, add more. Sauté until rice slightly browns. Remove from heat, add saffron, stock and cooked ingredients. Stir thoroughly, return to stove and bring to a boil. Add peas and chorizo; cook over low heat 15 minutes or until most of the liquid has been absorbed. Add shrimp and cook a few minutes until they turn pink. Serve hot, garnished with lemon wedges.

CHILLED SHELLFISH IN GREEN SAUCE

Serves 6

This fish can be prepared 6 hours ahead and sauce can be prepared 4 hours ahead, but let stand at room temperature.

2 cups water
8 uncooked unpeeled extra large shrimp
8 large mussels, scrubbed and debearded
8 large clams, scrubbed
2 tablespoons olive oil
1/4 cup minced onion
4 large garlic cloves, minced
2 teaspoons all-purpose flour
3/4 cup dry white wine
12 tablespoons minced fresh parsley
Salt and freshly ground pepper
Fresh lemon juice (optional)

<u>Fish</u>: Heat water in medium saucepan until just shaking, (beginning to boil). Add shrimp and cook until just opaque, about 2 minutes. Transfer shrimp to bowl using slotted spoon. Add mussels and clams to saucepan. Cover and steam over medium-high heat 5 minutes. Remove opened mussels and clams. Cook remaining mussels and clams about 5 minutes more; discard any that do not open. Ladle 1/2 cup poaching liquid through strainer lined with several layers of dampened cheesecloth; reserve. Peel and devein shrimp. Cover and refrigerate shrimp, mussels and clams.

<u>Sauce</u>: Heat oil in heavy skillet over medium heat. Add onion and garlic and cook until softened, stirring occasionally, about 5 minutes. Add flour and stir 1 minute. Mix in wine and 3 tablespoons parsley and bring to a simmer. Stir 3 minutes. Add reserved shellfish poaching liquid. Cover and simmer 15 minutes. Season sauce with salt and pepper. Mix in remaining parsley. Add lemon juice if desired. Cool.

Transfer sauce to serving dish. Set on platter. Arrange seafood around sauce and serve.

CIOPPINO

Serves 1
♥

4 tablespoons olive oil
1 onion, peeled and chopped
5 cloves garlic, peeled and chopped
2 green peppers, seeded and chopped
1/2 leek, chopped
1 1/2 cups canned Italian tomatoes
3/4 cup tomato purée
3/4 cup dry white wine
1 teaspoon dried basil
Salt and pepper to taste
12 ounces firm white fish, such as cod
8 ounces shrimp, shelled and deveined
8 ounces clams or oysters, shelled
4 tablespoons chopped fresh parsley

Garnish: Toasted garlic bread

Place olive oil, onion, garlic, green pepper, leek, tomatoes, and tomato purée in large pot. Cover and simmer 20 minutes.

Add wine, basil, salt, pepper and seafood. Cover and simmer another 10 minutes. Taste for seasoning.

Serve in soup bowls, garnished with parsley. Accompany with garlic bread.

FISH

MARYLAND CRAB CAKES WITH TARTAR SAUCE

Serves 5

Tartar Sauce
1 1/4 cup mayonnaise
1 teaspoon Dijon mustard
2 tablespoons minced parsley
3 tablespoons minced white onion
Juice of 1/2 lemon or to taste
2 tablespoons minced unsweetened pickles
1 tablespoon (or to taste) capers, drained, rinsed and minced
Salt and pepper to taste

Crab Cakes
2 cups crabmeat, cartilages removed
1 1/2 cups bread crumbs or as needed
1/2 cup fresh cream
3 tablespoons minced white onion
1 egg, room temperature
Salt and pepper to taste
1/8 teaspoon (or to taste) cayenne pepper
1 tablespoon (or to taste) lemon juice
3 tablespoons minced parsley
1 teaspoon paprika
Additional bread crumbs for coating
Butter as needed for frying

Garnish: Lemon wedges, fresh parsley or watercress sprigs

Tartar Sauce: Whisk all ingredients together. Taste for seasoning. Chill, covered, until ready to use.

Crab Cakes: Combine all ingredients in a bowl. Taste for seasoning. Shape into cakes and refrigerate, covered, until ready to use (at least 15 minutes). Coat with either bread crumbs or flour. Fry in butter until golden brown on each side and serve immediately, garnishing the plate with lemon wedges and parsley or watercress. Pass tartar sauce separately.

STEAMED HALIBUT WITH SPINACH AND BLACK OLIVE SAUCE

Serves 4

1/2 cup dry white wine
1/2 cup fish stock, bottled clam juice or canned low-salt
chicken broth
2 cups whipping cream
1 cup pitted black olives
Freshly ground pepper to taste
4 halibut fillets, 3/4 inch thick - 7 to 8 ounces each
3 tablespoons butter
8 ounces fresh spinach, stemmed
Salt to taste

Boil wine and stock in heavy medium saucepan until reduced to 1/4 cup. Add cream and olives. Lower heat and simmer until reduced to 2 cups, about 20 minutes. Cool slightly. Purée mixture in blender or food processor. Return to saucepan. Season with pepper.

Bring water to boil in base of steamer. Place fish on plate and arrange on steamer rack. Cover and cook until fish is just opaque, about 8 minutes.

Meanwhile, melt butter in heavy medium skillet over medium-high heat. Add spinach and stir until wilted, about 1 minute. Season with salt and pepper.

Stir sauce over medium heat until heated through. Divide sauce among plates. Top with bed of spinach. Place fish atop spinach and serve.

SALMON IN GINGER CILANTRO BUTTER SAUCE

Serves 4

Salmon Marinade
2 tablespoons soy sauce
2 tablespoons white wine or dry sherry
1/2 tablespoon sesame oil
2 teaspoons grated ginger
4 salmon fillets

Sauce
2/3 cup dry white wine
1/2 cup white wine vinegar
11/2 tablespoons finely minced ginger (or more, to taste)
1/4 cup finely minced white onion or shallot
1 cup unsalted butter, room temperature
11/2 teaspoons minced or grated lemon peel
1 cup minced cilantro (fresh corriander) or basil
Salt and white pepper to taste

Garnish: Sliver of fresh ginger

Combine ingredients for marinade. Marinate salmon at least 15 minutes.

In a small non-aluminum saucepan, place wine, vinegar, ginger and onion. Bring to a boil and cook down until just 3 tablespoons remain. Set aside. Prepare lemon and cilantro. Cut butter into small chunks and set aside unrefrigerated.

Grill or bake fish until done, brushing with any remaining marinade. Transfer fish to a heated platter or dinner plate.

Meanwhile, bring wine/vinegar sauce to a boil, add butter a little at a time, whisking continually. Turn heat off and add lemon and cilantro. Add salt and pepper to taste. Spoon around fish, top fish with slivered ginger and serve immediately.

GRILLED SALMON WITH GREEN PEPPERCORN BUTTER

Serves 4

4 tablespoons (1/2 stick) butter, softened
2 tablespoons green peppercorns, drained and chopped
1 teaspoon brandy
1/2 teaspoon dried parsley
4 salmon fillets (may substitute with tuna steaks)
2 tablespoons lemon juice
Olive oil
Salt and pepper to taste

Heat broiler.

Combine butter with peppercorns, adding brandy and parsley. Wrap in plastic wrap (in the shape of a log) and refrigerate until firm. This can be done earlier in the day.

Rub lemon juice into the fish on both sides. Salt and pepper to taste. Brush with oil. Broil until done. Top with a slice of flavored butter and serve immediately, on pre-warmed plates.

ROASTED SIDE OF SALMON WITH HERB VINAIGRETTE

Serves 6

♥

1 whole side of salmon (about 2 - 3 pounds)

Vinaigrette
1 cup olive oil
3 tablespoons seasoned rice wine vinegar
1/3 cup minced fresh herbs
    (dill, parsley, thyme, tarragon, marjoram)
Salt and pepper to taste

Potatoes and Vegetable
1 pound new potatoes, cut into eighth's
2 red bell peppers, seeded and cut into chunks

Heat oven to 375°

Combine vinaigrette ingredients and save half for potatoes and vegetables. Rub remaining half on salmon. Place salmon on oiled foil in a large baking pan. Bake 20-25 minutes for fish 1 1/4 - 1 1/2 inch thick.

Toss vegetables in half of remaining vinaigrette and place in roasting pan. Roast uncovered about 15 minutes until vegetables start to brown. Stir and cover pan. Bake until done (20-30 minutes more).

Remove salmon to platter and arrange vegetables around salmon. Pour remaining vinaigrette over all.

ROAST SALMON WITH LEEKS

Serves 4

3 large leeks, white parts only, cut into 1/4-inch slices (about 4 cups)
2 tablespoons water
1 tablespoon olive oil
1 teaspoon finely shredded lemon zest
2 teaspoons snipped fresh dill or 1/2 teaspoon dried dill weed
4 salmon steaks, 1/2 to 3/4 inch thick
1/2 teaspoon salt, or to taste
1/8 teaspoon coarsely ground black pepper, or to taste
2 tablespoons fresh lemon juice

Garnish: Sprigs fresh dill (optional)
    Lemon wedges

Heat oven to 425°

In a 13 x 9-inch baking dish, combine leeks, water, olive oil, zest and dill; stir to blend. Cover tightly with aluminum foil. Bake 20 minutes, stirring once after 10 minutes. Remove from oven.

Pushing leeks aside, arrange steaks in baking dish. Spoon leeks evenly over fish. Season with salt, pepper and lemon juice. Return to oven and bake uncovered, until salmon is opaque along center bone (15-20 minutes). Remove from oven and let stand 5 minutes.

Garnish with lemon wedges and dill (optional) before serving.

STEAMED ORIENTAL SNAPPER

Serves 4

1 Red Snapper about 11/2 - 2 pounds, cleaned, head on
1 tablespoon coarse salt
1 teaspoon ground ginger
1/2 teaspoon ground pepper
Snow peas and julienned carrots, blanched

Sauce
2 tablespoons olive oil
1 tablespoon fresh ginger, chopped
2 tablespoons chopped scallion (green onion)
1 tablespoon chopped garlic
1 teaspoon crushed red pepper flakes
2 tablespoons soy sauce
2 teaspoons balsamic vinegar
2 tablespoons sugar
1/2 cup water

Snapper: Make cross-hatch incisions in flesh of fish (about 5 each way) 1 inch deep on both sides of fish. Combine salt, ginger and pepper and rub into slash marks. Wrap fish in well-oiled heavy duty foil, sealing well, leaving air pocket at top. Bake at 425° until fish is completely cooked, 35 to 45 minutes.

Sauce: Heat oil in small sauce pan and add ginger, garlic, onion and pepper flakes. Do not allow pepper to burn. Add remaining ingredients and heat to dissolve sugar.

Remove fish to platter and place vegetables around fish. Pour sauce over fish.

BAKED FILLET OF SOLE WITH TOMATO, OREGANO AND HOT PEPPER

Serves 6

2/3 cup onion, very thinly sliced
3 tablespoons extra-virgin olive oil
1/2 teaspoon finely chopped garlic
1 cup canned Italian plum tomatoes, cut up, with juice
Salt to taste
2 tablespoons salt-packed capers, soaked and rinsed, or
   vinegar-packed capers, drained
2 teaspoons fresh oregano, or 1 teaspoon dried
Fresh black pepper or chopped hot red chilies, to taste
2 pounds gray sole fillets

Heat oven to 450°. Adjust oven rack to the top level.

Put onion and olive oil in a large skillet, turn heat to medium, and cook until the onion is golden. Add garlic, and saute until it turns pale gold; then add the tomatoes and a little salt, and stir. Simmer 20 minutes, until the oil floats on the surface of the mixture. Add the capers, oregano and pepper. Stir and cook a minute longer, and remove from heat.

Rinse and dry the fish. Select a baking dish large enough to hold the fillets folded in half lengthwise in a single layer. Spread a tablespoon of the tomato mixture in the bottom of the dish.

Dip each fillet into the tomato mixture to coat both sides, fold lengthwise, and arrange in baking dish. Pour remaining sauce over fish, and bake uncovered, 5 minutes or slightly longer, until fish is done.

Remove fish from the oven, tip the dish and spoon the sauce from the dish into a saucepan. Cook the sauce over high heat until it has returned to its original thickness. Spoon it back over the fish, and serve directly from the baking dish.

SPINACH SOLE WITH PESTO SAUCE

Serves 6

The sunny Italian flavor of the pesto-touched sauce combines well with Ratatouille, crusty French or Italian bread and a crisp green salad.

6 sole fillets, 6 to 7 ounces each
Salt and freshly ground pepper
1 cup dry white vermouth
1 tablespoon fresh lemon juice
2 tablespoons (1/4 stick) butter
1/4 cup chopped onion
1 garlic clove, minced
1 10-ounce package frozen chopped spinach, thawed and drained
3/4 cup freshly grated Parmesan cheese
1/2 teaspoon dried oregano
1 cup sour cream
1/4 cup pesto sauce (available dried or frozen) or see recipe
      on Page 75

Heat oven to 400°

Pat fish dry with paper towels. Place in single layer in two 9 x 13-inch baking dishes. Sprinkle with salt and pepper and cover with vermouth and lemon juice. Bake, covered, until fish loses its translucency, about 10-15 minutes. Pour off liquid and reserve. Remove fish and set aside to cool. Pour liquid into saucepan and reduce to 1/2 cup over medium-high heat.

Meanwhile, melt butter in medium skillet over moderate heat. Add onion and garlic and sauté until just golden. Turn into bowl. Add spinach, 1/4 cup Parmesan, oregano, salt and pepper and mix well (it will be quite thick). Return fillets to baking dishes. Divide spinach mixture over each, spreading evenly.

Add sour cream and pesto sauce to reduced liquid. Season to taste with salt and pepper. Spoon over fillets and sprinkle with remaining Parmesan. Dish may be covered and refrigerated at this point. Remove from refrigerator 2 hours before reheating.

Just before serving, preheat oven to 350°. Bake, uncovered, until heated through, about 5 to 10 minutes, then place under broiler several minutes until cheese is melted and bubbly.

130

PAN-SEARED TUNA WITH PINEAPPLE SALSA

Serves 1

♥

1 tuna steak per serving (6-8 ounces each)

<u>Marinade</u>
1/2 cup orange juice
1/4 cup soy sauce
2 cloves garlic
Oil for searing

<u>Pineapple Salsa</u>
2 cups very ripe, diced fresh pineapple
1/4 cup brown sugar
1 teaspoon rice vinegar
Chopped jalapeños to taste
1/2 cup diced sweet red bell pepper
Juice of 2 limes
2 tablespoons minced cilantro

Combine marinade ingredients. Allow tuna to marinate 1 hour to overnight. Remove and pat dry.

Heat oil to cover bottom of heavy skillet and sear tuna over high heat on both sides until medium rare and slice thin.

Combine salsa ingredients (does not keep well-use within 2 days). Serve sliced tuna with pineapple salsa.

131

MEAT

DAVID B. FINE

NOTES

STEAK TIPS WITH HORSERADISH SAUCE

Serves 25

Perfect party dish. The meat can be prepared a day ahead, but don't slice until ready to use. The sauce can also be prepared and chilled the night before.

Steak
9 large garlic cloves minced, or to taste
6 to 7 tablespoons oil
3 triangle tip roasts, 2 to 21/2 pounds each
Salt and freshly ground pepper

Horseradish Sauce
4 cups (2 pints) sour cream
1 cup white horseradish, drained
5 slices fresh white bread (crusts trimmed), torn into fine pieces
2 cups heavy cream

Heat oven to 400°

Combine garlic and oil. Rub thoroughly into meat and sprinkle generously with salt and pepper. Let roasts stand at room temperature for 2 to 3 hours.

Grill or broil meat very briefly, just to seal in juices. Transfer to rack set in roasting pan and roast to desired doneness, 45 to 60 minutes for medium-rare. Remove from oven and let cool. Wrap in foil and refrigerate overnight. Thinly slice and arrange on platter. Serve with Horseradish Sauce.

Sauce: Combine sour cream, horseradish and white bread in a large bowl and mash with fork to blend well. Stir 1/4 of the cream into horseradish mixture to loosen, then gently fold in remainder. Cover and refrigerate until ready to serve.

MARINATED FLANK STEAK

Serves 4

Marinade
1 tablespoon vegetable oil
1/2 cup soy sauce
1/4 cup red wine or sherry
1/4 cup fresh orange juice
1 teaspoon finely minced fresh ginger
2 cloves garlic, finely minced
Grated rind of 1 orange

1 to 2 pounds flank steak, room temperature

Combine all marinade ingredients and pour over steak. Cover and refrigerate overnight, or marinate 3 to 4 hours at room temperature. Barbecue or broil in oven, 10 minutes on each side. Slice thin and serve.

PEPPER STEAK

Serves 2

2 tablespoons Worcestershire sauce
1 tablespoon fresh lemon juice
1 tablespoon soy sauce
Dash pepper
1 tablespoon flour
1/2 cup water
1 tablespoon oil
1 pound round or flank steak, cut into 1 1/2-to 3-inch strips
1 green bell pepper, seeded and cut into slivers
1 cup chopped onion
1/2 cup chopped celery
1 (8 ounce) can tomato sauce
1/4 pound mushrooms, sliced (optional)
1/2 cup bean sprouts (optional)
Cooked white rice

Mix Worcestershire, lemon juice, soy sauce, pepper, flour and water. Marinate meat in mixture for a few hours. In a large skillet, sauté vegetables in hot oil until crisp-tender. Add meat and brown on both sides. Add tomato sauce, mushrooms and sprouts, stir, cover and simmer until tender. Serve with rice.

SPICY NUTTY BEEF

Serves 4 to 6

3 tablespoons chunky peanut butter
3 tablespoons dry sherry
2 tablespoons soy sauce
1 tablespoon chopped peeled fresh ginger
1 tablespoon chili powder
1 tablespoon sesame oil
1 teaspoon garlic salt
2 teaspoons sugar
1/2 teaspoon five-spice powder (optional)
Salt and freshly ground pepper
1 pound round steak, cut into 1-inch pieces
1 tablespoon vegetable oil
Freshly cooked rice

Combine first 9 ingredients in large bowl. Season with salt and pepper. Add beef, turning to coat. Refrigerate overnight.

Heat vegetable oil in a wok or large heavy skillet over medium heat. Add beef and the marinade and cook until beef is browned, stirring frequently, about 5 minutes. Serve hot, with rice.

SPICY BEEF AND VEGETABLE STIR-FRY

Serves 4

The vegetables, beef and peanuts can all be cut up or chopped ahead. The cornstarch mixture can also be prepared ahead.

1/2 cup regular or low-sodium beef broth
1 tablespoon regular or low-sodium soy sauce
2 teaspoons cornstarch
1 teaspoon Dijon mustard
2 teaspoons peanut oil
6 broccoli spears, cut into bite-size pieces
1 cup cauliflower florets
1/2 cup chopped onion
1 clove garlic, finely chopped
8 ounces cooked lean roast beef, cut into strips
1 ounce unsalted peanuts, coarsely chopped
1/4 teaspoon crushed red pepper flakes
1/4 teaspoon fresh ground black pepper

In a small bowl, combine the beef broth, soy sauce, cornstarch, and mustard, and stir until the cornstarch is dissolved. Set aside.

In a nonstick wok or large nonstick skillet, heat the oil over medium-high heat until hot but not smoking. Add the broccoli, cauliflower, onion, and garlic, and stir-fry until the vegetables are crisp-tender and the onion begins to brown, 4 to 5 minutes.

Stir the cornstarch mixture again and pour it into the wok. Stir in the beef, peanuts, red pepper flakes, and black pepper, and stir-fry until the sauce thickens and the beef is heated through, 2 to 3 minutes. If necessary, reduce the heat to keep the sauce from evaporating.

HEARTY BEEF STEW

Serves 4 to 6

2 teaspoons minced garlic
1 1/2 teaspoons salt
2 pounds lean beef round, cut into 1-inch cubes
3 cups finely chopped onions
1/2 teaspoon dried thyme
1/2 teaspoon pepper
1 (28 ounce) can whole tomatoes
2 tablespoons tomato paste
2 pounds red potatoes, cut into small pieces
2 pounds carrots, peeled and cut into small slices
1 pound small mushrooms
1 package (10 ounces) frozen peas, thawed

Heat oven to 325°

With flat side of knife, crush garlic with salt to make a paste. In Dutch oven, combine garlic paste, beef, onion, thyme and pepper. Cover and roast 1 1/2 hours, or until meat is tender.

Stir in tomatoes, tomato paste, potatoes, carrots and mushrooms, and cook 1 1/2 hours. Stir in peas and heat through. Serve.

CARAWAY BEEF STEW

Serves 8

This dish can be prepared the night before and then reheated.

1/2 cup (1 stick) butter or margarine
3 pounds chuck, sirloin or top round, cut into 1-inch cubes
1 dozen medium onions, sliced
2 tablespoons sweet paprika
1 tablespoon caraway seeds
1 tablespoon dried marjoram
2 teaspoons salt
Juice of half a lemon
1 large garlic clove, crushed (optional)
1/2 cup dry red wine
1 tablespoon flour
1 tablespoon tomato paste

Garnish: Chopped parsley

In a large stewpot or Dutch oven, melt butter until it bubbles. Add meat all at once, turning until cooked on all sides. Mix in onion and half each of paprika, caraway, marjoram, salt and lemon juice. Add garlic clove, if desired, and wine. Stirring occasionally, simmer uncovered until meat is tender, about 1 1/2 to 2 hours.

Blend in remaining paprika, caraway, marjoram, salt, lemon juice, and flour mixed with tomato paste and a bit of liquid from the stew. Simmer 15 minutes more. Garnish stew with parsley.

FAVORITE CHILI

Serves 4

The longer this dish sits in the refrigerator, the better it tastes.

3 pounds ground beef
2 or 3 medium onions, chopped
1 bell pepper, seeded and chopped
1 or 2 cloves garlic, minced or crushed
1/2 teaspoon dried oregano
Salt and pepper to taste
At least 3 tablespoons chili powder
2 (15 ounce) cans pinto beans
1/4 teaspoon cumin seeds
2 (6 ounce) cans tomato paste (or, if you prefer canned tomatoes,
  put them through a colander)

Brown beef in an iron kettle or large heavy skillet. Continue cooking while adding onion, pepper and garlic to the browned meat. Then add oregano, cumin seeds, tomato paste or tomatoes, and about 1 quart of water. Salt liberally and grind in some black pepper and the chili powder (to taste). Bring to a boil and simmer for another 1/2 hour. Remove from heat and let sit for several hours. Heat to serve.

BEEF

LUCY'S FAMOUS MEAT LOAF

Yield: 2 loaves-10 servings

3 tablespoons or more olive oil
1 large onion, peeled and diced
2 celery stalks, diced
3 to 4 large cloves garlic, minced
2 teaspoons each dried basil, oregano and thyme
2 pounds lean ground beef
7 to 8 ounces chorizo sausage, roughly chopped
1 (28 ounce) can Italian whole tomatoes, drained and chopped
1 (6 ounce) can tomato paste
1 small green bell pepper, seeded and diced
1/2 cup minced Italian flat or curly parsley
1 egg, lightly beaten
1/2 to 3/4 cup bread crumbs
1 teaspoon or more black pepper

Heat oil in heavy pan. Sauté onion, celery, garlic, basil, oregano and thyme. Cover and cook until vegetables are very tender, stirring often. Transfer to large bowl and cool slightly.

Mix beef and sausage into vegetable mix. Add tomatoes, tomato paste, green pepper, parsley, egg, bread crumbs and pepper; mix well. (Easiest way is with hands.)

Heat oven to 350°

Lightly grease 2 loaf pans with olive oil. Divide mix and press into pans, making loaf shapes. Bake about 45 to 60 minutes. Pour off any accumulated fat. Cool slightly in pans.

To serve: Remove loaves from pans and place on platter.

STEAKS WITH BRANDY, SHALLOT & MUSTARD SAUCE

Serves 2

This recipe can be doubled or tripled.

3 tablespoons butter
1 tablespoon vegetable oil
2 pieces filet mignon, 1 to 11/4 inches thick
Salt and freshly ground pepper
2 large shallots, sliced
3 tablespoons brandy
1 cup unsalted beef stock
1/2 teaspoon Dijon mustard

Garnish: Snipped fresh chives

Melt 1 tablespoon butter with oil in large heavy skillet over medium-high heat. Season steaks with salt and pepper. Add to skillet and cook 2 minutes per side to sear. Reduce heat to medium and cook to desired degree of doneness. Transfer steaks to heated platter. Cover; keep warm.

Wipe out skillet. Add 1 tablespoon butter and melt over medium heat. Add shallot and sauté 1 minute. Remove from heat; cool 1 minute. Add brandy and ignite with match. When flames subside, add stock and boil over high heat until syrupy, about 8 minutes. Whisk in mustard and remaining 1 tablespoon butter. Adjust seasoning. Spoon sauce over steaks. Garnish with snipped chives and serve.

BREAST OF VEAL STUFFED WITH DRIED FRUIT AND HERBS

Serves 6
♥

Have the butcher bone, trim and butterfly the veal breast for you.

1 14-pound veal breast, boned, trimmed and butterflied
Salt and freshly ground white pepper
Stuffing
2/3 cup dried pitted prunes
2/3 cup dried apricots
2/3 cup raisins
1 cup cooking sherry
3 tablespoons unsalted butter
2 medium carrots, peeled and diced
2 celery stalks, diced
1 large onion, diced
3/4 pound mushrooms, minced
2 bay leaves
1/2 teaspoon minced fresh thyme or pinch of dried, crumbled
3 medium garlic cloves, pressed
1/2 teaspoon minced fresh rosemary or pinch of dried, crumbled
1/2 teaspoon minced fresh tarragon or pinch of dried, crumbled
1/2 teaspoon minced fresh marjoram or pinch of dried, crumbled
Salt and freshly ground pepper

Using mallet or rolling pin, pound veal to thickness of 1/3 inch. Season with salt and pepper. Cover with plastic and refrigerate while preparing stuffing.

For stuffing: Soak fruit in sherry in small bowl until softened, about 15 minutes. Drain fruit, reserving sherry. Coarsely chop fruit and place in large bowl. Melt 2 tablespoons butter in large heavy skillet over medium heat. Add carrot, celery and onion and cook until vegetables are tender, stirring frequently, about 10 minutes. Add to fruit. Melt remaining 1 tablespoon butter in same skillet over medium heat. Add mushrooms, bay leaves and thyme and cook 10 minutes, stirring frequently. Increase heat to high. Add reserved sherry and stir until almost all liquid evaporates, about 5 minutes. Add to vegetables in bowl. Mix in garlic and remaining herbs. Season with salt and pepper. (Can be prepared one day ahead; chill.)

Arrange veal, boned side up, on work surface. Spread stuffing over, leaving 1-inch border on each long side. Starting at one short end, roll veal jelly-roll style. Tie with string to secure. Place in large roasting pan seam side down. Refrigerate 1 hour.

Heat oven to 350°. Roast veal until tender, about 21/2 hours. Place on platter; let stand 20 minutes. Degrease pan juices (skim off fat).

ROSEMARY-SCENTED VEAL WITH CROOK-NECK SQUASH & SUN-DRIED TOMATOES

Serves 4
♥

1/3 cup coarsely chopped marinated sun-dried tomatoes (about 4), 3 tablespoons oil reserved
1 pound boned veal leg, cut into 2 x 1/2-inch slices, patted dry
2 tablespoons olive oil
1/2 medium red onion, coarsely chopped
1 clove garlic, minced
1/4 teaspoon crushed red pepper flakes
1 1/4 pounds crookneck squash, halved if large and thinly sliced
1/3 cup chicken stock
3 tablespoons dry white wine
1 teaspoon instant flour
1 1/2 teaspoons minced fresh rosemary
1/2 to 3/4 teaspoon coarse salt
Freshly ground pepper to taste
2 tablespoons chopped fresh parsley
2 teaspoons fresh lemon juice

Heat reserved sun-dried tomato oil in large heavy skillet or wok over medium-high heat. Add veal and stir until opaque on all sides, a few minutes. Remove from skillet. Heat olive oil in same skillet. Add onion, garlic and pepper flakes and stir 10 seconds.

Add tomatoes and squash and stir 30 seconds. Remove from skillet. Blend in stock, wine and flour and cook until reduced by half, about 1 minute. Add rosemary and cook 1 minute. Mix in salt. Season with pepper. Return veal-and-squash mixture to skillet. Cook until veal is done. Add parsley and lemon juice and toss to heat through. Serve immediately.

VEAL NORMANDE

Serves 4 to 6

You can substitute 6 chicken breast halves, skinned, boned and pounded.

11/2 **tablespoons butter or margarine**
11/2 **tablespoons olive oil**
6 thinly sliced veal cutlets, pounded
5 tablespoons brandy
1/2 teaspoon chopped shallot
1 (101/2**-ounce) can cream of mushroom soup**
2/3 cup milk
1 tart medium apple, peeled, cored and thinly sliced
Freshly cooked wild rice

Melt butter with oil in large skillet over medium-high heat. Add veal and brown, turning once. Transfer to platter. Add brandy and shallot to skillet and stir, scraping up any browned bits clinging to bottom of pan. Blend in soup and milk.

Return veal to pan with apple. Reduce heat and simmer, stirring once or twice, until heated through. Serve over rice.

VEAL RAGOÛT WITH RED PEPPER

Serves 8

A do-ahead stew with the flavors of osso buco, the classic Italian dish made with veal shanks and vegetables.

5 tablespoons olive oil
3 pounds veal stew meat, cut into 11/2-inch pieces, trimmed
1/2 cup chopped carrot
1/2 cup chopped onion
1/4 cup all-purpose flour
4 cups chicken stock
1 (28-ounce) can Italian plum tomatoes, drained
1 cup dry white wine
3 parsley sprigs
2 medium garlic cloves, crushed
1 bay leaf, crumbled
1 teaspoon dried thyme, crumbled
1/2 teaspoon dried basil, crumbled
Salt and freshly ground pepper
1 large red bell pepper, seeded and cut into 1-inch squares
1/2 cup chopped fresh parsley
1/4 cup minced scallion (green onion)
2 teaspoons minced garlic
2 teaspoons grated lemon peel
2 pounds fresh fettuccine
3 tablespoons butter

Heat the oil in heavy Dutch oven over medium-high heat. Pat veal dry. Add to pan in batches (do not crowd) and cook until brown on all sides, adding more oil if necessary, about 10 minutes. Drain on paper towels. Add carrot and onion to pan and cook 5 minutes, stirring frequently. Return veal to pan; sprinkle with flour. Cook, stirring for 3 minutes. Add stock and bring to boil, scraping up any browned bits. Mix in tomatoes, wine, parsley sprigs, crushed garlic, bay leaf, thyme, basil, salt and pepper. Bring to simmer, stirring constantly and breaking up tomatoes. Reduce heat, cover and simmer about 1 hour. Uncover and simmer until veal is tender, about 20 minutes longer.

Add bell pepper and cook until just tender, about 10 minutes. Transfer meat and bell pepper to bowl, using slotted spoon. Discard parsley. Skim surface of cooking liquid. Boil until reduced to 2 cups, stirring occasionally, about 20 minutes. Return meat and pepper to pan. Combine chopped parsley, scallion, minced garlic and lemon peel. Cook fettuccine in boiling salted water until just tender but still firm. Drain well. Return to pot and mix with butter. Arrange around outer edge of large deep platter. Spoon ragoût into center of platter.

LAMB WITH FRESH DILL SAUCE

Serves 4 to 5

2 pounds lamb cut in 2 pieces, rinsed lightly in cold water
    and patted dry
Water as needed
1 1/2 teaspoons salt, or as needed
10 peppercorns
1 peeled carrot, cut in half
1 leek, cut in half

Sauce
2 tablespoons butter
2 tablespoons flour
8 ounces strained lamb stock
2 tablespoons fresh lemon juice
4 tablespoons minced fresh dill
1/2 cup fresh cream
1 egg yolk
Salt and pepper to taste

Garnish: Fresh dill

Place the lamb (cut in two) in a soup pot. Cover with water. Add salt and bring to a boil. Skim off scum. Add peppercorns, carrot and leek. Turn heat down to a high simmer and cover. Cook until lamb is tender and still slightly pink inside, about 45 minutes; remove lamb from pot. Strain off 1 cup of stock for sauce. Keep the meat hot.

Sauce: In a saucepan, melt the butter and stir in flour until blended. Add the stock and whisk constantly until thickened. Boil for 3 minutes. Add lemon juice and dill. Turn heat off. Mix the cream and egg yolk together. Add to sauce and stir. Season to taste. Reheat gently, not boiling, until sauce is very hot. Slice lamb into thin slices. Place on plate. Garnish with dill and serve immediately. Ladle sauce lightly over the lamb and pass remaining sauce separately.

LAMB IN PASTRY WITH MINT PESTO

Serves 4

<u>Mint Pesto</u>
1 1/4 cups washed, chopped fresh mint leaves, stems removed
1 large clove garlic, peeled and minced
1/4 cup olive oil
Salt and freshly ground black pepper to taste

8 thick lamb chops
1 large package frozen puff pastry, thawed
1 egg yolk, beaten

Garnish: Fresh mint
      Mint jelly (optional)

Heat oven to 400°

Make Mint Pesto by puréeing mint, garlic, olive oil and seasonings in food processor or blender. Place in small bowl and set aside.

Trim any excess fat off lamb. Season to taste with salt and pepper. Roll out puff pastry into fairly thin squares. Cut into 8 pieces, each big enough to enclose 1 lamb chop.

Place 1 tablespoon Mint Pesto in center of each square and top with 1 lamb chop. Top with another spoonful of Mint Pesto and fold over to enclose lamb. Using a little water, crimp edges together firmly. Brush top of pastries all over with beaten egg. Bake until puff pastry is golden brown and meat is medium-rare, roughly 10-15 minutes. Garnish with mint leaves and serve piping hot, with mint jelly if desired.

GRILLED LAMB WITH BALSAMIC VINEGAR SAUCE

Serves 4

Sauce
1/2 cup dry white wine
3 rosemary sprigs
1 1/2 teaspoons balsamic vinegar
1 1/2 teaspoons minced shallot
1/4 teaspoon cracked black pepper
2 cups veal, lamb or beef stock

Lamb
1/4 cup red currant jelly
1/2 teaspoon minced fresh rosemary
1/8 teaspoon minced garlic
1 18-ounce boned lamb loin, trimmed
Coarse salt
Coarsely ground pepper

3 tablespoons unsalted butter, room temperature

Sauce: Boil wine, rosemary, vinegar, shallot and pepper in heavy medium skillet until reduced to 2 tablespoons, about 6 minutes. Add stock and boil until reduced to 5 tablespoons, about 25 minutes. (Can be prepared 6 hours ahead and refrigerated.)

Lamb: Prepare barbecue grill on medium heat, or preheat oven to 350°. For marinade, combine jelly, rosemary and garlic in glass baking dish. Season lamb with salt and pepper. Add to marinade, turning to coat. Marinate 10 minutes.

Grill or bake lamb until cooked to desired degree of doneness, about 5 minutes per side for rare. Transfer to platter.

Return sauce to boil. Reduce heat to low and whisk in butter, 1 tablespoon at a time. Strain sauce. Season with salt and pepper. Spoon sauce onto plates. Slice lamb and arrange atop sauce.

BROILED LAMB CHOPS WITH MUSTARD

Serves 4

3/4 cup plain bread crumbs
1/2 cup fresh parsley, minced
1 tablespoon minced fresh thyme or rosemary or
    1/2 tablespoon dried
5 tablespoons or more olive oil
2 tablespoons Dijon mustard
1 teaspoon minced garlic
Salt and pepper to taste
8 rib lamb chops

Heat broiler. Mix all ingredients together in bowl, except lamb. Spread mixture onto both sides of chops. Broil until done, turning once. Be careful not to burn. Serve immediately.

GREEK LAMB STEW

Serves 4
♥

3 tablespoons olive oil
2 pounds leg of lamb, cut into cubes
2 medium onions, peeled and thinly sliced
Dried thyme flakes to taste
Salt and black pepper to taste
1/2 to 3/4 cup dry white wine
1 (10 ounce) package frozen artichoke hearts, defrosted
Juice of 1 lemon
1/2 teaspoon dried anise seed or to taste
1/2 teaspoon dried dill weed or to taste
Cooked white rice

Sauté lamb, onion, thyme, salt and pepper in the olive oil in a deep pan. Add the wine, and simmer covered until tender (approximately 30 minutes).

Add the artichoke hearts, lemon juice, anise and dill and cook until heated through. Serve with plain white rice.

149

PORK

GRILLED PORK TENDERLOIN WITH RED PEPPERS AND BALSAMIC VINEGAR

Serves 4

2 pork tenderloins (about 1 pound total)
Salt, freshly ground black pepper and paprika to taste
3 to 5 tablespoons butter
1 tablespoon olive oil
1 pound roasted red peppers, peeled (or from a jar is OK)
1 medium onion, very thinly sliced
1 tablespoon balsamic vinegar
1/2 cup red wine
1/2 cup chicken broth or veal stock

Garnish: 2 scallions (green onions), sliced thin

Heat oven to 400°.

Dry the pork with a paper towel. Place it on a piece of waxed paper; season with salt, pepper and paprika to taste.

In a skillet large enough to hold the two pork tenderloins, heat 1 tablespoon butter and the oil over high heat. When the butter foam subsides, brown the pork in the pan on all sides, about 6 minutes.

Meanwhile, cut the peppers into long slices. (If using peppers from a jar, rinse and drain them well.) Remove the pork and set it aside. Add the onion and red pepper to the pan and cook for 5 minutes, until the onion browns lightly and becomes limp. Add the vinegar, wine and broth to the pan. Boil the mixture for 2 minutes, then return the pork to the pan and put the pan in the oven. Roast the pork for approximately 25 minutes, until done.

Remove the pan from the oven and let it stand for 5 minutes before serving.

To serve, remove the pork to a cutting board. Swirl the remaining butter into the mixture in the pan. Divide the mixture in the pan among four plates. Cut the pork into 3/4-inch slices and divide among the four plates, as well. Sprinkle sliced scallion over the top and serve.

PORK CHOPS IN LIME CREAM SAUCE

Serves 6

6 lean pork chops
1 tablespoon vegetable oil

Sauce
2 tablespoons unsalted butter
4 tablespoons minced white onion
1/2 cup dry white wine
1 1/2 cups chicken broth
8 ounces heavy cream
Juice of 1 large lime
Salt and black pepper to taste

Garnish: Lime-peel slivers

Sauce: Melt butter in large skillet and sauté onion until soft. Add wine and boil until reduced by half. Add chicken broth and boil until reduced by half. Add cream and boil for about 5 minutes, stirring frequently. Turn heat off and add lime juice, salt and pepper.

Just before serving, sauté the pork chops in oil until done, seasoning to taste. Place sauce on plate, top with pork chop and garnish with lime peel. Serve immediately.

PORK IN MUSHROOM-CREAM SAUCE

Serves 4

4 lean pork chops
2 eggplants, cubed
Salt and pepper to taste
Oil and butter as needed
4 tablespoons minced onion
1 large garlic clove, minced
6 or more shiitake mushrooms, coarsely chopped
1 pack Shimedi or other mushrooms, coarsely chopped
4 tablespoons dry white wine
8 ounces heavy cream
2 teaspoons Dijon mustard
Lemon juice to taste

Garnish: Minced scallion (green onion)

Season pork to taste with salt and pepper. Sauté eggplant in a little oil and butter and season to taste with salt and pepper. Set aside. Add more oil and butter to pan. Cook pork to desired doneness. Set aside.

Add more oil and butter to pan and sauté onion and garlic. Add mushrooms and wine and cook over medium heat until soft. Add cream and mustard; season to taste with salt and pepper. Cook for an additional few minutes to thicken. Add pork and lemon juice and cook briefly. Serve pork with sauce on top. Garnish with scallion.

PORK

PORK CHOPS PROVENCALE

Serves 4

4 thick pork chops, trimmed
Salt and pepper to taste
2 tablespoons or more olive oil
1 1/2 teaspoons dried rosemary
1 1/2 teaspoons dried thyme
Dashes dried tarragon and basil
3 tablespoons minced onion
1 tablespoon or more minced garlic
1 1/2 tablespoons red wine vinegar
1 tablespoon red wine
1 (28 ounce) can whole Italian tomatoes, chopped
1 large tomato, diced
1 bay leaf
Dash crushed red pepper flakes
1/4 cup or more small pitted black olives

Garnish: Chopped fresh basil or parsley

Salt and pepper pork chops. In large skillet, heat the olive oil. Cook chops on one side until brown; turn over. Sprinkle both sides with herbs while cooking, reserving some of the rosemary and thyme for sauce. Remove chops and cover to keep warm.

Drain off most of the fat in pan; add onion and garlic. Cook until slightly browned. Add remainder of dried herbs, vinegar, wine, tomatoes, bay leaf, red pepper flakes, black olives, salt and pepper. Cover and simmer 5 minutes.

Add any juices from meat. Turn heat up and reduce sauce slightly. Taste for seasoning. Remove bay leaf and spoon sauce over chops. Garnish with basil or parsley and serve immediately.

153

PORK

BARBECUED PORK SPARERIBS

Yield: 3 cups

You can substitute beef ribs if desired.

12 pork spareribs on bone

Sauce
2 cups ketchup
1/4 cup Dijon mustard
3 tablespoons brown sugar
3 tablespoons hoisin sauce
3 tablespoons fresh lemon juice
2 tablespoons white vinegar
1 tablespoon Tabasco sauce
Grated peel from 1/2 lemon
3 to 4 cloves garlic, peeled and minced

Mix all sauce ingredients together in bowl. Marinate ribs in sauce for up to 24 hours in refrigerator.

Heat oven to 350°

Grill or oven-bake ribs until well done. If baking, place ribs on well-oiled baking sheet or on aluminum foil and bake in marinade. If grilling, brush ribs with sauce as often as possible.

Serve hot.

PORK WITH MUSTARD COATING

Serves 4

3/4 cup bread crumbs
1/2 cup minced fresh parsley
1 tablespoon minced fresh thyme or 1/2 tablespoon dried
5 tablespoons olive oil (or more if needed)
2 tablespoons Dijon mustard
Salt and pepper to taste
1 teaspoon minced garlic
4 thick pork chops or pork tenderloin

Heat oven to 375°

Mix all the ingredients together in a bowl, except for the meat. Pat some of the mixture onto both sides of the meat.

Bake until done. Turn once. Be careful not to burn. Serve immediately.

Vegetables

DAVID B. FINE

NOTES

156

STUFFED ARTICHOKES

Serves 4 to 6

4 large or 6 medium artichokes
3/4 cup plain bread crumbs
1/3 cup freshly grated Parmesan cheese
1/4 cup chopped fresh parsley
3 cloves garlic, minced or crushed
1/2 teaspoon salt
Pepper to taste
2/3 cup olive oil

Heat oven to 350°

Using a sharp knife, cut off the top third of each artichoke and the tough stem. With kitchen shears, cut off the pointed tops of the remaining leaves. Pull off the small discolored leaves around the base of the artichokes.

Cook artichokes in a covered large pot of boiling salted water 10 minutes. Drain and cool. Remove the fuzzy chokes and small inner leaves with a small spoon (a serrated grapefruit spoon works well), making sure to scrape out all the fuzz.

Mix the remaining ingredients. Stuff mixture into center and between the leaves of the artichokes. Place them in a baking dish and pour 1 inch of boiling water around their bases. Lightly cover with foil. Bake 20 minutes. Remove the foil and bake 10 minutes more. Serve hot.

VEGETABLES

SAUTÉED GREEN APPLES AND LEEKS

Serves 4

2 large leeks, white part only
2 tablespoons unsalted butter
2 large green apples such as Granny Smith, cored, quartered,
   and thinly sliced

Split leeks in half lengthwise, leaving a little of the root end intact so they stay together. Wash well and dry. Cut leeks into thin strips about 2 inches long.

In a medium sauté pan over medium heat, melt 1 tablespoon butter. Add leek and cook until soft, about 3 minutes. Remove from pan and set aside.

Melt remaining tablespoon butter and add apple slices. Turn heat to high and cook until apples are lightly browned and soft, about 3 minutes. Return leeks to pan and toss together to combine. Serve immediately.

BRUSSEL SPROUTS WITH BACON & PECANS

Serves 4

1 pint brussel sprouts, washed and cored
5 slices bacon
2 teaspoons vegetable oil, used only if necessary
1/4 cup pecans, chopped
2 scallions (green onions), minced
Nutmeg to taste
Salt and pepper to taste

Shred brussel sprouts in food processor. Fry bacon until crisp; drain on paper towel and dice. If needed, add vegetable oil to remaining bacon fat, then sauté pecans until slightly browned. Add sprouts, scallions and nutmeg. Cook, stirring frequently, until crisp-tender. Just before serving, stir in bacon and taste for seasoning.

RED CABBAGE

Serves 6

1 large onion, diced
2 tablespoons butter or margarine
2 large apples, cubed
1/4 to 1/2 cup cider vinegar
1/4 cup brown sugar
1/2 cup golden raisins
6 peppercorns
1 1/2 pounds red cabbage, shredded
Salt and pepper to taste
2 teaspoons caraway seeds

Sauté onion in butter or margarine until soft. Add apples, vinegar, brown sugar, raisins and peppercorns; stir.

Add shredded cabbage. Cook slowly on a low flame in tightly covered pot, stirring occasionally with a slotted spoon, for 1 hour, or until cabbage is tender. Add caraway seeds after cooking for 1/2 hour. Adjust seasoning.

RED AND GREEN CABBAGE WITH BACON AND BLUE CHEESE

Serves 6

8 ounces thick-sliced bacon
1/2 cup olive oil
1 small red cabbage, cored and thinly sliced
1/2 green cabbage, cored and thinly sliced
1 clove garlic, peeled and minced
2 to 3 large shallots (or 6 tablespoons finely diced
   white onion), chopped
1/8 to 1/4 cup red wine vinegar
Salt and pepper to taste
3 tablespoons dried parsley

Garnish: 4 ounces crumbled blue cheese

Sauté bacon until crisp in medium-sized skillet. Place bacon on paper towels to drain. Chop bacon. Reserve 1 tablespoon bacon fat in skillet. Add half of olive oil to bacon fat in skillet; add cabbages and sauté until they start to wilt. Remove to serving bowl.

Add remaining oil, garlic and shallot to skillet. Sauté briefly over medium-high heat. Add vinegar, salt and pepper to taste and dried parsley. Taste for seasoning. Add bacon and reheat slightly.

Pour hot dressing over cabbage and toss. Top with blue cheese. Serve hot or warm.

CARROTS MARGUERITE

Serves 4

3 shallots, finely minced
1/4 cup (1/2 stick) butter
1 pound carrots, peeled and shredded
3 tablespoons honey
1/2 teaspoon dried thyme
1/4 teaspoon salt
Dash freshly ground pepper

Sauté shallots in butter a few minutes over low heat, until soft and just turning golden. Add carrots, honey, thyme, salt and pepper.

Stir over medium heat to coat carrots evenly. Cover and cook 3 minutes. Serve immediately.

SAUTÉED CARROTS AND APRICOTS

Serves 4 to 6

5 tablespoons unsalted butter
1 medium onion, cut into thin strips
1 pound carrots, shredded
4 ounces dried apricots, cut into thin strips
1/2 cup stock or water
1 to 2 teaspoons sherry vinegar (imported Spanish preferred)
Salt and freshly ground pepper

Melt butter in large skillet over medium-high heat. Add onion and cook until browned. Add carrots and apricots and stir-fry about 2 minutes.

Stir in stock and cook, covered, until carrots are crisp-tender, about 5 minutes. Uncover and cook until all liquid evaporates. Season with vinegar and salt and pepper to taste.

EGGPLANT SAUTÉ WITH GOAT CHEESE AND BASIL

Serves 4

Serve hot or at room temperature on spinach fettuccine.

1/4 cup plus 1 tablespoon olive oil
1/4 pound carrots, peeled and cut into 3 x 1/8-inch strips
1/2 pound eggplant, peeled and cut into 3 x 1/4-inch strips
2 tablespoons water
1 teaspoon coarse salt
1/2 small red onion, coarsely chopped
2 garlic cloves, minced
1/4 teaspoon crushed red pepper flakes
1 pound Italian plum tomatoes, peeled, seeded and quartered
2 tablespoons dry white or red wine
1 tablespoon balsamic vinegar
1/2 cup chopped fresh basil leaves
3 tablespoons pine nuts, toasted
Freshly ground pepper
4 ounces goat cheese

Heat 1/4 cup oil in large heavy skillet or wok over high heat. Add carrots and stir 45 seconds. Add eggplant and stir 2 minutes. Add water and stir 1 minute. Transfer to bowl. Toss with 1/2 teaspoon salt.

Heat remaining tablespoon of oil in same skillet over high heat. Add onion, garlic and pepper flakes and stir 10 seconds. Add tomatoes and cook 10 seconds. Add remaining 1/2 teaspoon salt and wine and cook until sauce thickens, about 11/2 minutes. Remove from heat.

Stir in carrot-eggplant mixture, vinegar, basil and pine nuts. Season with pepper. Spoon onto plates immediately, or let stand 10 minutes. Crumble goat cheese over each serving.

VEGETARIAN CHILI

Serves 2
♥

1 large eggplant, peeled and cubed
1 large onion, chopped
1 medium red bell pepper, chopped
1 medium green bell pepper, chopped
3 tablespoons olive oil
1 (15 ounce) can kidney beans
1 package chili seasoning
1 (28 ounce) can whole tomatoes, drained and mashed,
  juice reserved
2 carrots, peeled and diced

In a large stockpot, sauté the eggplant, onion and peppers in olive oil about 10 to 15 minutes (you may want to cover pot, as the eggplant sticks).

When eggplant is translucent, mix in beans and seasonings and stir for a few minutes. Stir in tomatoes slowly. Put in half of the reserved tomato juice. Simmer for at least 10 minutes. Serve with rice, grated cheese and sour cream.

UN-MEAT BALLS

Serves 10

For the vegetarian in your life.

1/2 cup ground walnuts
3/4 cup whole-wheat bread crumbs
1 tablespoon fresh parsley, chopped
1 medium onion, chopped
1 tablespoon fresh sage or 1 teaspoon dried
3 eggs, beaten
Oil for frying

Mix ingredients together. With a tablespoon, form into balls with your hands. Place in well-heated, oiled skillet and fry; be sure to brown on all sides.

SAUTÉED SHIITAKE MUSHROOMS WITH GARLIC, OLIVE OIL AND RED PEPPER

Serves 4

2 packages dried shiitake mushrooms, washed and coarsely sliced
1/4 cup plus 2 tablespoons olive oil
4 garlic cloves, peeled and coarsely chopped
1 dried red pepper, finely chopped
1/4 cup fresh parsley, finely chopped
1/2 cup plain bread crumbs
Salt and pepper to taste

Garnish: Lemon wedges

Marinate the mushrooms in 1/4 cup olive oil with garlic for 15 minutes.

In a large pan, sauté the mushrooms, garlic and red pepper in the olive oil. Add the remaining 2 tablespoons of oil. Cook until the garlic gets crispy. At the last moment stir in parsley and bread crumbs and cook until the bread crumbs turn brown. Taste for seasoning.

Garnish with lemon wedges and serve immediately.

164

GOLDEN ONION RINGS

Serves 6

2 large red onions, peeled and thinly sliced
2 large white onions, peeled and thinly sliced
2 cups all-purpose flour
1 1/4 teaspoons cayenne or more to taste
2 tablespoons paprika or more to taste
Salt and black pepper to taste
Oil for frying
2 eggs, beaten

Separate onions into rings; mix together and set aside.

Mix flour and seasonings in bowl. Heat oil in either a wok or heavy saucepan.

Dredge onion rings in flour, shake off excess, dip in beaten eggs and then once again in the flour. Shake off excess. Fry until golden brown. Drain on paper towels and keep warm until all onion rings are cooked.

Serve immediately.

CHORIZO-STUFFED SWEET PEPPERS

Serves 6
🕒

3 chorizos, chopped
Olive oil as needed
1 medium onion, chopped
1 medium tomato, chopped
2 cups cooked hot white rice
1 egg, beaten
1 tablespoon minced fresh parsley
Salt and pepper to taste
6 orange or red bell peppers, parboiled in salted water,
    drained and cooled
Bread crumbs as needed

Heat oven to 350°

Sauté the chorizo in a little oil until browned. Add the onion and tomato, cooking until softened. Turn heat off; add rice, egg and parsley. Season to taste with salt and pepper.

Core and seed peppers; cut off tops to stuff. Generously stuff the peppers, topping with the bread crumbs and a dab of oil. Bake for 15 minutes, or until golden brown. Serve very hot.

FRIED GREEN TOMATOES

Serves 6

3 large green tomatoes, cored
3/4 cup unsifted self-rising flour
1 tablespoon salt
1/4 teaspoon pepper
Vegetable oil as needed (corn, safflower or canola, etc.)
3 tablespoons bacon grease

Cut tomatoes into 3/8-inch-thick slices. On waxed paper, mix flour with salt and pepper. Coat tomatoes with mixture and let sit 15 minutes.

In cast-iron or other heavy skillet, heat 1/2 inch oil and the bacon grease over medium-high heat. Lightly recoat tomatoes with flour mixture; brown on both sides, 3 minutes in all. Serve hot.

RED TOMATO SAUTÉ

Serves 4

1 tablespoon butter
1 tablespoon olive oil
2 cloves garlic, peeled and minced
3 cups red cherry tomatoes, stemmed
Salt and pepper to taste

Garnish: 1 tablespoon minced parsley
*   1 tablespoon perilla leaves*

Sauté garlic in butter and olive oil over low heat. Add tomatoes and increase heat; quickly sauté, shaking pan, for a few minutes. Season to taste with salt and pepper. Place in serving bowl and toss with parsley and perilla leaves. Serve immediately.

SPINACH LOAF

Serves 6

1/2 cup minced onion
4 minced cloves garlic
1 (2 ounce) can anchovy fillets, drained and chopped
1/4 cup olive oil
1 cup white rice
4 (10 ounce) packages frozen leaf spinach, defrosted
and drained
1/2 cup grated Parmesan cheese
1 tablespoon dried parsley flakes
1 teaspoon salt
1/2 teaspoon ground black pepper
Dash garlic powder
1 egg, beaten
2 cups Italian bread crumbs

Cook rice and set aside.

In a small skillet sauté onion, garlic and anchovies in olive oil over medium heat for 10 minutes. Remove from heat and cool.

Heat oven to 350°.

In a large bowl, combine rice, spinach and onion mixture with cheese, parsley, salt, pepper, garlic powder and egg. Blend well. Add enough bread crumbs so that mixture will hold together. Shape the spinach mixture into a loaf and place in a greased 13 x 9 x 2-inch baking pan. Bake 1 hour. Slice to serve.

SPICED ACORN SQUASH

Serves 12

♥

6 acorn squash, about 1 pound each
3/4 teaspoon ground cinnamon
3/4 teaspoon ground ginger
1/4 teaspoon ground mace
1 tablespoon brown sugar
6 tablespoons low-fat butter substitute, melted (or less)
1 tablespoon apple cider vinegar

Heat oven to 350°

Split each squash in half lengthwise; scoop out and discard seeds and fiber from centers. Slice a piece from the underside of each half so it rests flat. Place, cut sides up, in a shallow baking dish.

Mix spices together; sprinkle over squash. Sprinkle with brown sugar.

Combine melted butter substitute with vinegar; drizzle over squash. Cover pan tightly with foil and bake for 13/4 hours.

Remove foil; baste with juices from cavities. Return to oven for 10 minutes. Remove and serve.

VEGETABLE LOAF

Serves 4 to 6

This vegetable loaf is perfect with a white sauce. (See Sauce Section.)

1 cup sliced onion
1/2 pound sliced mushrooms
2 cloves garlic, minced
2 tablespoons vegetable oil
1/2 tablespoon dried basil
1/4 teaspoon dried thyme
1/2 teaspoon salt
1/4 teaspoon pepper
3 cups grated carrot (about 1/2 pound)
3/4 cup grated cheddar cheese
3/4 cup bread crumbs
3 eggs, lightly beaten
2 tablespoons butter

Heat oven to 350°

In a large skillet over low heat, sauté the onion, mushrooms and garlic in the vegetable oil. When the onion is soft and transparent, add the basil, thyme, salt and pepper. Stir and set aside.

In a large bowl, combine the carrot, 1/2 cup of cheddar cheese, 1/2 cup of bread crumbs and eggs. Add the onion sauté to this and mix together well. Shape into a loaf with your hands. Carefully place the loaf in a medium buttered baking dish.

Melt the 2 tablespoons butter in a skillet and add 1/4 cup bread crumbs. Stir until the crumbs are coated. Sprinkle the coated crumbs and remaining 1/4 cup of cheddar cheese over the loaf. Cover it with aluminum foil and bake for 30 minutes. Remove the foil and bake, uncovered, for 10 minutes more, or until the topping has turned brown.

STIR-FRIED VEGETABLES WITH HERBES DE PROVENCE

Serves 6

2 bunches asparagus, trimmed and cut into 2-inch lengths,
    quickly parboiled
1 package snow peas, ends removed and quickly parboiled
1 package fresh shiitake mushrooms, stemmed and cut
    into strips
1/2 pound green beans, ends removed and quickly parboiled
3 tablespoons peanut oil
1 box cherry tomatoes, stemmed
Dried tarragon to taste
Pinch each dried basil and thyme
Salt and pepper to taste

Garnish: Freshly grated Parmesan cheese

In a large skillet or wok, quickly stir-fry asparagus, snow peas, mushrooms and green beans in peanut oil. Just before serving, add tomatoes; stir gently to cook. All vegetables should be crispy. Flavor with tarragon, basil, thyme and salt and pepper to taste. Sprinkle lightly with Parmesan cheese and serve immediately.

VEGETABLE SAUTÉ

Serves 6 to 8

♥

1 large red bell pepper
1 large green bell pepper
1 large yellow bell pepper
1/2 pound button mushrooms, washed and thickly sliced
1/2 cup snow peas, washed, stemmed and parboiled
1/2 cup green beans, washed, stemmed and cut diagonally
1 to 2 bunches green asparagus, diagonally cut and parboiled
2 tablespoons butter or olive oil
2 to 3 tablespoons chopped fresh basil
Salt and pepper to taste

Seed, derib and julienne all peppers. Heat butter in skillet and sauté all vegetables (except asparagus and snow peas) over medium heat until cooked but still somewhat firm. Add asparagus, snow peas, basil, salt and pepper to taste. Cook briefly and serve.

ZUCCHINI-AND-TOMATO CASSEROLE

Serves 8 to 10

6 to 8 medium zucchini, washed and sliced crosswise
6 to 8 medium tomatoes, sliced
1 large sweet onion, sliced
1 1/2 cups cornflake crumbs
1 cup grated sharp cheese
Salt and pepper
1/4 pound (1 stick) butter, cut into small pieces
1 tablespoon brown sugar

Heat oven to 350°

Alternate layers of zucchini, tomatoes, and onion in a large buttered casserole, sprinkling each layer with crumbs, cheese, salt and pepper and dotting with bits of butter.

Sprinkle the brown sugar over the tomato layers. The top layer should be cheese.

Bake for 1 hour and 15 minutes.

ZUCCHINI ITALIANO

Serves 4

♥

3 tablespoons olive oil
2 small white onions, chopped
1 garlic clove, mashed
1 pound firm, 1 1/2-inch-diameter zucchini, cut into 1/4-inch slices
1 teaspoon seasoned salt
1/4 teaspoon dried oregano

Combine oil, onion and garlic in a large skillet and cook 3 minutes on high. Stir in zucchini and season with salt and oregano. Cover and cook 3 minutes on high, stirring.

Lower heat and cook an additional 3 minutes. Stir. Let stand, covered, 5 minutes before serving.

NOTES

CONFETTI MASHED POTATOES

Serves 6 to 8

This recipe can be prepared 1 day ahead. Cover and refrigerate.

7 medium russet potatoes, peeled
1/2 cup milk
1/4 cup (1/2 stick) butter, room temperature
1 8-ounce package cream cheese, cut into chunks, room temp.
1/2 cup chopped scallion (green onion)
1 (2-ounce) jar chopped pimientos, well drained
Salt and freshly ground pepper
1 egg, beaten

Heat oven to 350°

Place potatoes in large saucepan. Cover with cold water and boil until tender. Drain. Mash potatoes with milk and butter in large bowl. Mix in cream cheese, scallion and pimientos. Season with salt and pepper. Stir in egg.

Transfer potatoes to 9 x 13-inch glass baking dish. Bake until puffed and light brown, about 25 minutes.

POTATO GNOCCHI

Makes about 60

If dusted with flour, gnocchi can be frozen for up to 1 month in an airtight container. They will keep in the refrigerator for up to 1 week.

2 pounds potatoes, boiled, peeled and quartered
1-2 tablespoons butter, softened
1 1/2 cups flour
1 egg
Nutmeg to taste
Salt and pepper to taste

Mash potatoes in a large bowl. Add butter and blend well. Slowly add flour, egg, nutmeg, salt and pepper to potatoes. With your hands, work into a dough. You want a slightly firm but still soft dough.

In a pan coated with flour, roll out dough into thick logs and cut on the bias. Touch top of each piece with a fork to make a slight indent. Boil in salted water until the gnocchi start to float. Serve immediately.

POTATO-AND-PARSNIP PUDDING

Serves 8

3 pounds potatoes, boiled, peeled and quartered
1 pound parsnips, peeled and cut into chunks
4 tablespoons (1/2 stick) butter or margarine
3 cups chopped onion
3 tablespoons flour
3 large eggs, beaten
Salt and pepper to taste
1/8 teaspoon nutmeg

Heat oven to 400°

Cook potatoes and parsnips in a large pot of boiling water until tender. Drain and mash. Sauté onion in melted butter or margarine until translucent.

Grease a 2 1/2-to 3-quart baking dish and coat with flour. Mix onion, eggs and seasonings into potato mixture. Pack into baking dish. Bake 45 to 60 minutes, until top is brown.

POTATOES

SWEET POTATOES ANNA

Serves 6

5 medium sweet potatoes, peeled and sliced 1/8 inch thick
6 tablespoons (3/4 stick) melted butter
2 slender leeks, white parts only, washed and cut in half lengthwise
and then into thin slices
1 tablespoon dried thyme
Salt and pepper to taste

Heat oven to 375°

Butter a shallow round 10-inch baking dish. Arrange a layer of potatoes in overlapping circles. Brush with 1/4 of melted butter. Top with half of leeks and half of thyme and salt and pepper. Repeat another layer of potatoes and remaining leeks and thyme. Top with final layer of best-looking potato slices. Brush with melted butter.

Cover pan with aluminum foil. Put a heavy skillet or baking dish on top to press potatoes into a compact mass. Bake 30 minutes. Remove foil and baste with remaining butter. Continue baking for about 30 minutes, until potatoes are very soft and the top and bottom layers have started to caramelize. If potatoes begin to char, cover with foil. Cool for 15 minutes before serving.

SWEET POTATOES WITH APRICOTS AND PRUNES

Serves 6 to 8
♥

4 medium sweet potatoes, peeled
1/3 cup pitted prunes
1/4 cup dried apricot halves
2 cups apple cider
1 tablespoon butter

Heat oven to 350°

Cut the sweet potatoes into large cubes. Place in medium oven-proof casserole dish with lid.

Add the remaining ingredients. Push the prunes and apricots down so that they are covered with liquid. Cover the casserole.

Bake for 1 hour, stirring once or twice during baking. To serve, carefully drain the hot liquid from the casserole into a small saucepan. Keep the casserole hot as you boil down the liquid to half it's volume over medium-high heat. Pour the sauce over the sweet potatoes and serve hot.

SWEET POTATO-PECAN PIE

Yield: 1 9-inch pie

Potato Filling
1 cup roasted, peeled and mashed sweet potatoes
1/4 cup packed brown sugar
2 teaspoons sugar
1 egg, lightly beaten
1 teaspoon unsalted butter, softened
1 teaspoon vanilla extract
1/4 teaspoon salt
1/4 teaspoon ground cinnamon
1/8 teaspoon ground allspice
1/8 teaspoon ground nutmeg

Pecan Filling
3/4 cup granulated sugar
3/4 cup dark corn syrup
2 eggs
11/2 teaspoons vanilla extract
1/8 teaspoon salt
1/8 teaspoon ground cinnamon

Pie
1 9-inch unbaked pie shell
3/4 cup pecan halves, chopped
3 ounces semi-sweet chocolate melted
3 tablespoons heavy cream
Whipped cream (optional)

Heat oven to 350°

Sweet-potato filling: Combine all the ingredients in a mixing bowl. Beat with an electric mixer on medium speed until smooth, about 2 to 3 minutes. Set aside.

Pecan filling: Combine all ingredients in a mixing bowl and beat for 1 minute.

Spoon the sweet-potato filling into the pie shell. Pour the pecan filling over that. Sprinkle with the pecans. Bake until a knife inserted into the center of the pie comes out clean, about 40 minutes. Let cool.

Combine the melted chocolate and the cream. Cut the pie into slices, drizzle with the chocolate mixture and serve, topped with whipped cream, if desired.

COCONUT RICE

3 cups boiling water
1 1/2 cups shredded fresh or unsweetened dry coconut*
3 tablespoons butter
1 onion, chopped
1 1/2 cups long-grain rice
1 teaspoon salt
1 teaspoon ground cardamom

Garnish: Toasted shredded coconut

Pour boiling water over coconut. Let stand 20 minutes. Strain through double thickness of cheesecloth to extract as much liquid as possible. Reserve coconut liquid.

Melt butter in large heavy skillet over medium heat. Add onion and cook until golden, stirring occasionally, about 5 minutes. Add rice and stir until color begins to change, 3 to 4 minutes.

Add coconut liquid and bring to boil. Blend in salt and cardamom. Reduce heat to low, cover and cook until rice is tender and all liquid is absorbed, about 20 minutes. Garnish with toasted coconut and serve.

* Available at natural-food stores

CURRIED RICE

Serves 8 to 10

2 large onions, sliced
4 cloves garlic, minced
3 tablespoons butter or margarine
4-inch cinnamon stick
3 cardamom pods, cracked
1 bay leaf
1 teaspoon salt
1/3 teaspoon grand turmeric
2 cups uncooked rice
4 cups water
Garnish: 2 hard-cooked eggs, sliced
*   1/4 cup raisins*
*   1/4 cup toasted almonds, sliced*

Heat butter in a 2-quart saucepan. Cook onion and garlic covered, until tender but not brown. Add cinnamon, cardamom, bay leaf, salt, turmeric and rice. Cook for 5 minutes. Do not brown. Stir in water, bring to boil and cover. Cook on low heat for 20 minutes. Remove bay leaf. Let stand for 10 minutes. Garnish with eggs, raisins and almonds.

LEMON CAPER RICE WITH PARSLEY

Serves 6
♥

2 cups uncooked rice
4 to 5 tablespoons butter
Salt and pepper to taste
Juice of 1/2 lemon
1 to 2 tablespoons drained and minced capers
4 tablespoons chopped fresh parsley

Cook rice. Add a little less water than usual to make slightly firmer. Heat 1/2 of butter in a wok. Add cooked rice, salt, pepper, lemon juice and capers; stir well. Add remaining butter and blend well. Remove from heat and stir in parsley. Taste for seasoning and serve immediately.

RICE WITH BLACK-BEAN SAUCE

Serves 4

If there are no canned black beans in your market, soak 2 cups dried black beans in water overnight. Drain, add water to cover, and simmer until tender. Serve with roast chicken or pork.

3 tablespoons butter
1 onion, chopped
3 garlic cloves, minced
1 (16-ounce) can black beans, drained
1/2 cup canned beef broth
1 bay leaf
Salt and pepper
1 cup white rice, freshly cooked

Melt butter in heavy medium saucepan over medium-high heat. Add onion and garlic and cook until soft, stirring occasionally, about 7 minutes.

Stir in black beans, broth and bay leaf. Season with salt and pepper. Reduce heat. Cover and simmer until thick, stirring frequently, about 25 minutes.

Remove bay leaf. Serve immediately over rice.

PECAN-AND-WILD RICE PILAF

Serves 6
♥

3/4 cup uncooked brown rice
1/4 cup uncooked wild rice
2 cups chicken stock
1 small onion, peeled
1 whole clove garlic
2 tablespoons finely grated carrot
1 shallot, finely minced
1 tablespoon butter
1 cup pecan halves

Place rices, stock, onion, garlic, carrot and shallot in a medium saucepan. Bring to a boil, then reduce heat as low as possible; cover and steam 50 minutes.

Remove from heat and keep covered. Melt the butter in a medium skillet and lightly brown the pecans. Remove the onion and garlic from the rice. Toss the rice, then stir in the pecans. Serve hot.

SESAME-WILD RICE CAKES

Serves 4
🕐

1 egg
1 teaspoon Worcestershire sauce
1 teaspoon cumin powder
Pinch salt
3 tablespoons sesame oil
Juice of 1 lime
1/2 cup flour
1 cup wild rice, cooked

Combine all ingredients except rice and 2 tablespoons of sesame oil; and blend until smooth. Mix in the rice. Form into silver dollar sized cakes. Heat remaining sesame oil in large frying pan. Fry cakes until brown on both sides.

BLACK BEANS, SAUSAGE AND RICE

Serves 6 to 8

1 pound dry black beans
6 cups water
1 cup chopped onion
1 medium green bell pepper, chopped
1 clove garlic, minced
3 tablespoons olive or vegetable oil
1 pound hot Italian or Polish sausage, cut in 1-inch pieces
1 bay leaf
1 teaspoon ground cumin
1 teaspoon sugar
1 teaspoon salt
1 cup uncooked rice

Wash and sort beans. Combine beans and water in large saucepan. Bring to a boil and cook 2 minutes. Remove from heat, cover and let stand 1 hour. Then simmer about 1 hour. Set aside.

In medium frying pan, cook onion, pepper and garlic in oil until tender but not brown. Add sausage; brown on all sides. Add sausage mixture and seasonings to beans. Continue cooking another hour, covered, or until beans are tender.

Meanwhile, cook rice in separate saucepan. Serve beans over rice.

RISOTTO WITH HAM AND ASPARAGUS

Serves 4

1/2 cup smoked ham or prosciutto
6 to 8 scallions (green onions)
2 bunches asparagus
6 cups chicken stock, preferably homemade
3/4 cup dry white wine
4 tablespoons (1/2 stick) butter
11/2 cups rice, arborio or any short-grain type
3 to 4 tablespoons minced chervil or fresh parsley
1 cup chopped fresh tomatoes
Salt and pepper

Cut ham into thin strips. Cut scallions, including some of the green tops, into thin slices. Trim asparagus and cut stalks into 1-inch pieces.

In a medium pot, heat stock and wine. Add asparagus and simmer until just tender, about 4 minutes. Remove asparagus with slotted spoon and reserve liquid.

Melt butter in heavy saucepan. Sauté ham until golden brown and remove. Add rice and cook, stirring, 1 to 2 minutes. Cover rice with stock (1 cup); simmer over medium heat, stirring constantly. Add additional stock only when previous stock has been absorbed. Total cooking time is about 30 minutes. Cover pot for last 10 minutes to speed up cooking and help soften rice. When done, rice should be tender but firm.

At last moment, add cooked ham, asparagus, minced chervil and tomatoes. Heat through; season with salt and pepper. Serve immediately.

DR. SHELLEY'S SUNDAY BEANS

Serves 12
♥

Beans can also be mashed and served with tortillas and salsa.

6 cups pinto beans
2 medium onions, finely chopped
3 cloves garlic, finely chopped
1 stalk celery, finely chopped
1/2 bell pepper, finely chopped
1 carrot, finely chopped
1 apple, peeled and finely chopped
1 jalapeño pepper, seeded and finely chopped
1 bay leaf
1/2 pound bacon, cut into small pieces
1 1/2 teaspoons salt (or to taste)

Sort through the beans and clean. Place them in a large pot, cover with water, and let soak overnight. Drain and cover with water once more.

Add the remaining ingredients and bring to a simmer. Cook for 3 hours, or until beans are very soft, adding water as needed to keep beans covered by about 1 inch.

Remove bay leaf. Serve with rice and corn bread.

NOTES

CHAWAN MUSHI (JAPANESE CUSTARD)

Serves 4
♥

4 eggs, beaten
3 1/2 cups chicken stock
4 ounces cooked chicken, minced
4 ounces cooked shrimp, minced
4 dried minced mushrooms, soaked in water until soft
1/2 cup spinach leaves, chopped

Combine eggs with stock. Pour into 4 custard cups and add chicken, shrimp, and mushrooms. Place in steamer (boiling water up to 1/2 height of cups). Steam for 20 minutes. Add spinach; steam 5 minutes more. Serve warm.

DEVILED EGGS

Serves 4

4 large eggs, hard-boiled and peeled
1 teaspoon Dijon mustard
1 tablespoon minced fresh parsley
2 teaspoons drained, rinsed, chopped capers
1 tablespoon fresh lemon juice
1 tablespoon oil
White pepper to taste
4 anchovy fillets, drained and halved (optional)

Garnish: Watercress

Cut eggs lengthwise. Carefully remove yolks and mash them in a small bowl. Add all other ingredients, except anchovies. Taste for seasoning. Pile egg-yolk mixture back into egg whites.

Garnish each with 1/2 anchovy fillet, placed in the center. Place deviled eggs on bed of watercress and serve with crackers.

WELSH RAREBIT WITH CRISP BACON

Serves 4

2 tablespoons unsalted butter
2 1/2 tablespoons white flour
1 cup beer (not dark), or more if needed to thin out cheese
2 cups grated sharp cheddar cheese
1/2 teaspoon dry mustard
1 teaspoon Worcestershire sauce
1/4 teaspoon Tabasco sauce, or more
Black or white pepper to taste
4 English muffins, split and toasted
8 slices crisp bacon, drained on paper towels

Garnish: Parsley sprigs

In medium saucepan, melt butter over low heat and add flour. Stir constantly, about 3 minutes, to make a roux. Whisk in beer and bring to a boil, whisking continually, about 3 to 4 minutes.

Reduce heat to low; add cheddar cheese, mustard, Worcestershire sauce, Tabasco and pepper to taste. Cook but do not boil, until cheese has melted and mixture is hot. Taste for seasoning.

Place two muffin halves on each plate and spoon cheese sauce over. Place two slices bacon on side and garnish with parsley. Serve immediately.

SHRIMP QUICHE

Serves 6 to 8

Quiche goes great with salad and wine. Or serve as an hors d'oeuvre.

3 eggs
1 cup light cream or half-and-half
3/4 cup shredded Gruyère or Swiss cheese
1/2 teaspoon salt
1 cup thinly sliced white onion
1/2 stick (4 tablespoons) butter
1/2 teaspoon dried marjoram
1/4 cup dry sherry
1 pound small shrimp, cooked, peeled and deveined
1 unbaked 9-inch pastry shell (deep dish)

Heat oven to 350°.

Mix eggs, cream, cheese and salt. Set aside. Sauté onion in butter on low heat until soft but not brown. Add onion to the egg mixture and combine with marjoram, sherry and shrimp.

Bake pastry shell about 5 minutes before filling to brown bottom.

Spoon mixture into pie crust and bake 30 to 35 minutes.

ZUCCHINI FRITTATA

Serves 4

2 tablespoons olive oil
2 medium zucchini, grated (with skin)
4 eggs, beaten
1/4 teaspoon each pepper, dried basil, oregano and thyme
3/4 cup grated cheddar cheese

Garnish: Chopped tomato
Parmesan cheese

Quickly fry zucchini in oil and transfer to mixing bowl. Add all other ingredients to bowl and stir together. Drop 1/4 cupful into still-hot skillet. Cook until eggs begin to set, then flip once. Continue cooking until eggs are fully set.

Serve hot or cold, with chopped tomato and grated Parmesan.

SCRAMBLED EGGS WITH HERBS

Serves 4

6 large eggs, room temperature
2 ounces cream cheese, softened and cubed
3 tablespoons minced scallion (green onion)
2 tablespoons heavy cream
Salt and pepper to taste
1 tablespoon dried parsley flakes
1/4 teaspoon dried oregano
1/4 teaspoon dried basil
Dash dried tarragon
2₁/₂ tablespoons butter or margarine

Garnish: Minced fresh parsley

Beat the eggs with the cream cheese, scallion, cream and seasonings.

Melt butter in large skillet until sizzling. Scramble egg mixture over medium heat until softly set. Place on serving plate or individual plates and sprinkle parsley on top. Serve hot.

SWISS CHEESE FONDUE

Serves 1

1/2 pound cheese mix (before removing rind), grated or cut into
    cubes*
1 clove garlic, crushed
1 1/2 ounces dry or medium-dry white wine
1 teaspoon Kirsch
1 teaspoon cornstarch
Pinch dry mustard
Pinch white pepper
Pinch baking soda

*Cheese Mix - 65% Gruyère, 25% Tilsit, 10% Vacheron Fribourgh
(In a pinch, you can use 100% Gruyère)

To grated or cubed cheese, add garlic and wine. Melt cheese in fondue pot
over medium heat, stirring with wooden spoon in one direction only. Mix in
Kirsch, cornstarch, mustard and pepper.

Just before serving, add the baking soda to the surface. Serve by putting
fondue pot over alcohol burner to keep cheese bubbling during meal. Dip
in small pieces of crusty French bread, apples or items of choice.

VEGETABLE FRITTATA

Serves 4 to 6

2 tablespoons butter
1 cup corn kernels, fresh, canned or frozen
1 cup diced cooked carrots
1 cup cooked and drained chopped spinach, fresh or frozen
Salt and pepper
7 eggs
1/2 cup grated Gruyère or Swiss cheese
1/4 cup shredded fresh basil leaves
1/2 cup grated Parmesan cheese

Heat a large round platter in a 150° oven.

Melt butter in a 10-to 12-inch skillet, preferably nonstick. Add the vegetables, season with salt and pepper and cook gently for about 5 minutes.

Beat together the eggs and cheeses and season the mixture with salt and pepper. Pour over the vegetables in the skillet, sprinkle with the basil and cook slowly over low heat. Lift the edges gently so the uncooked mixture flows underneath, but try not to actually stir it too much.

Total cooking time is about 5 to 7 minutes, or until the frittata is lightly browned on the bottom and the top is still quite moist but not runny and raw. Invert the frittata onto the warm platter-which will cook the top-and serve hot, warm or cold, sprinkled with Parmesan cheese and cut into wedges.

desserts

DAVID B. FINE

NOTES

APPLE WALNUT CAKE

Serves 14

3 cups all-purpose flour
2 cups granulated sugar
1 1/4 cups oil
1/2 cup orange juice
4 large eggs
1 teaspoon salt
3 teaspoons ground cinnamon
1 teaspoon baking soda
1 1/2 teaspoons vanilla extract
10 to 12 apples (Macs or Delicious) peeled, cored and
*   thinly sliced*
1 cup chopped walnuts

Heat oven to 350°

Flour a large tube pan and grease well. Combine all ingredients except nuts and apples. Place in mixer and blend on medium speed until batter is thick, 3 to 5 minutes (if too thick, add more orange juice). Add apples and nuts and mix.

Pour into pan, fill but not to brim and bake for 60 to 75 minutes (check cake after 50 minutes) or until toothpick inserted in center comes out clean. Let cool.

BLACKBERRY-CORN MUFFIN CAKE

Serves 8 to 10

A dense, moist cake with a muffinlike tenderness. Can be made with firm raspberries or blueberries.

Cake
2 cups unbleached all-purpose flour
1 cup yellow cornmeal
2 teaspoons baking powder
1/4 teaspoon salt
3/4 cup (1 1/2 sticks) unsalted butter, room temperature
1 1/2 cups sugar
2 tablespoons minced orange peel
3 large eggs, room temperature
1 1/2 cups buttermilk
3 cups fresh blackberries or frozen, unsweetened, unthawed

Glaze
3 tablespoons sugar
1/3 cup orange marmalade
3 tablespoons unsalted butter
1 1/2 tablespoons heavy cream

Garnish: Additional fresh blackberries (optional)

Heat oven to 375°

Cake: Butter and flour a 12-cup nonstick ring or Bundt pan. Mix first 4 ingredients in medium bowl. Using electric mixer, cream butter with sugar and orange peel in large bowl until light and fluffy. Blend in eggs 1 at a time. Fold in half of the dry ingredients. Stir in buttermilk and blackberries. Gently fold in remaining dry ingredients.

Spoon batter into prepared pan. Bake until cake begins to pull away from sides of pan and tester inserted in center comes out clean, about 50 minutes. Cool cake in pan on rack for 15 minutes.

Glaze: Melt butter, sugar and marmalade. Add heavy cream; simmer until well combined, about 2 minutes. Then pour over cooled cake and garnish with fresh blackberries.

CHOCOLATE CREAM CAKE

Serves 6

4 eggs
1 cup sugar
1 cup all-purpose flour
7/8 cup heavy cream or crème fraîche
4 ounces bittersweet chocolate, grated

Heat oven to 375°

Butter an 8-inch round cake pan that is at least 2 inches deep, or use an 8-inch springform pan.

In a mixing bowl, beat the eggs and sugar until the mixture is very smooth. Mix in the flour. Stir in the cream and chocolate.

Transfer the batter to the prepared pan and bake for 45 minutes. Let the cake cool in the pan for 10 minutes, then turn the cake out onto a rack to cool completely.

FLOURLESS CHOCOLATE CAKE

Serves 8

10 ounces semi-sweet chocolate chips
31/2 ounces unsalted butter
7 eggs, separated
1/3 cup confectioners sugar

Heat oven to 250°

Melt chocolate with butter in top of double boiler (or microwave oven). Cool to room temperature.

Beat egg whites until stiff. Stir egg yolks into chocolate mixture. Fold in egg whites. Pour into greased and floured 9-inch springform pan. Bake for 1 hour and 15 minutes. Cool for 15 minutes. Remove sides of pan. Sprinkle with confectioners sugar on top.

GERMAN APPLE CAKE

Serves 6 to 8

This recipe has an easy-to-make crust that can also be used as cookie dough. You will have enough dough left over for another use.

Dough
1 cup granulated sugar
1 large egg
2 cups (4 sticks) butter or margarine, softened
3 cups all-purpose flour
Apple Cake Filling
4 to 5 large baking apples
1/2 cup unseasoned bread crumbs
1 cup sour cream
1/2 cup heavy cream
1/2 cup granulated sugar
2 large eggs
Juice of 1 lemon
1 tablespoon cornstarch
1/4 teaspoon vanilla extract
1/2 cup apricot preserves

Crust: In a large bowl, combine the sugar, egg, butter, and flour. Using your fingertips, work the mixture together until it is of pastry consistency. Cover the dough and refrigerate for at least 1 hour, or until slightly firm.

Cake: Preheat oven to 375°. Lightly butter a 9-inch springform pan. Dust lightly with flour and tap out any excess. Press half of the dough into the pan, covering the bottom and reaching about halfway up the sides. (Save the remaining dough for another use.)

Peel the apples. Core, and cut them in half. Using the point of a small knife, cut small strips on top of the apples to score them. Sprinkle the bottom of the crust with the bread crumbs to form a thin, even layer. Arrange the apples, rounded sides up, on the top. Fill in any empty spaces with pieces of apple.

In a large bowl, stir together the sour cream, heavy cream, sugar, eggs, lemon juice, cornstarch, and vanilla. Pour this mixture over the apples. Bake for 60-90 minutes, or until the apples are tender and the filling is set. Remove the pan from the oven and set on a wire rack to cool. Cool completely before removing from the pan.

In a small saucepan, heat the apricot preserves over medium heat until warm. When the cake has cooled slightly, brush the preserves over the top to form a glaze.

SOUR-CREAM COFFEE CAKE WITH PECAN STREUSEL

Serves 6

1/4 cup firmly packed brown sugar
2 tablespoons rolled oats
1/2 teaspoon ground cinnamon
2 tablespoons (1/4 stick) butter, cut into pieces
2 tablespoons chopped pecans
12/3 cups all-purpose flour
1 teaspoon baking powder
1 teaspoon baking soda
1/2 teaspoon salt
1 cup granulated sugar
1/2 cup solid vegetable shortening
2 eggs
1 cup sour cream
1 teaspoon vanilla extract
1 egg white, room temperature
1/3 cup plum jam, room temperature

Heat oven to 350°

Butter an 8-inch square baking pan. Combine brown sugar, oats and cinnamon in bowl. Cut in butter until mixture crumbles. Mix in nuts. Set streusel aside.

Sift together flour, baking powder, baking soda and salt. Using electric mixer, beat 1 cup sugar and shortening in large bowl until fluffy, about 4 minutes. Add eggs, 1 at a time, beating well after each addition. Stir in sour cream and vanilla. Add flour mixture and stir just until blended.

Beat egg white in another bowl until stiff but not dry. Gently fold in plum jam, 1 tablespoon at a time.

Spoon half of batter into buttered pan, spreading evenly. Sprinkle with half of streusel. Spoon egg-white mixture over top in dollops; do not spread. Spoon remaining batter over, distributing evenly but allowing some egg-white mixture to show through. Sprinkle with remaining streusel.

Bake until toothpick inserted in center comes out clean, about 55 minutes. Serve warm.

YELLOW POUND CAKE

Serves 8 to 10

Cake
1 package yellow cake mix
1 package instant vanilla pudding
1/3 cup vegetable oil
1 cup water
4 eggs

Glaze
1/3 cup melted butter
2 cups confectioners sugar
1 1/2 teaspoons vanilla extract
2 - 4 tablespoons hot water

Heat oven to 350°

Cake: Grease and flour a Bundt pan. Blend all cake ingredients in a large bowl. Beat at medium speed for 2 minutes. Bake for 50 to 60 minutes. Cool cake in pan for 25 minutes, then remove from pan. Top with glaze when completely cool.

Glaze: Combine all ingredients except hot water. Stir in water 1 teaspoon at a time until desired consistency is achieved.

PECAN-RUM TEA CAKE

Serves 8 to 10

Makes one 9 x 2-inch round or one 10 1/2 x 15 1/2 x 3/4-inch rectangle (for roll). Round pan bakes for 25 minutes; rectangle for 15 - 17 minutes.

4 eggs
1/3 cup light brown sugar
1 teaspoon vanilla extract (fruit-flavor extracts make good
*   substitutes)*
Pinch salt
1/3 cup plus 1 tablespoon granulated sugar
1 cup ground nuts
1/2 cup flour
4 tablespoons (1/2 stick) unsalted butter, melted and cooled
2 tablespoons water
3 tablespoons rum
2/3 cup confectioners sugar

Garnish: Pecan halves

Heat oven to 350°

Butter cake pan, line bottom with waxed or parchment paper and butter the paper.

Separate 3 eggs; place yolks and whites in separate bowls. Add the remaining whole egg to the yolks and beat at medium speed until blended. Slowly beat in the brown sugar and then the vanilla extract. Continue beating at high speed until the mixture is very light, about 3 minutes. Clean and dry beaters.

Add salt to egg whites and beat at medium speed until the whites are opaque and just begin to hold their shape. Increase the speed to high and gradually beat in the 1/3 cup of granulated sugar. Continue beating until the whites are glossy and hold firm peaks.

Using a large rubber spatula, gently fold the whites into the yolk mixture. Stir the ground nuts to aerate them and then pour them on one side of the egg mixture. Fold in the ground nuts until half incorporated (mixed). Sift the flour over the batter and continue folding just until the batter is smooth; be careful not to deflate the batter by overmixing.

(Continued on Page 204.)

DESSERTS

PECAN-RUM TEA CAKE (cont'd)

In a small bowl, gently stir 1/2 cup of the batter into the melted butter, then fold it into the remaining batter until mixed. Scrape the batter into the prepared pan, smoothing the surface with a metal spatula. Bake until cake is light golden about 45 minutes, and a toothpick inserted in the center comes out clean.

Loosen the cake from the pan with the point of a small sharp knife. Invert the cake on a rack, remove the pan and peel off the paper. Cover the cake with another rack and turn it right side up. Let cool to room temperature.

In a small saucepan, combine the 1 tablespoon granulated sugar and water and bring to a boil, stirring to dissolve the sugar. Remove from heat and let cool, then stir in 1 tablespoon rum.

While cake is still warm, brush the rum syrup evenly over the top. Let cake cool completely.

In small saucepan, combine confectioners sugar and remaining 2 tablespoons rum. Stir until smooth. Place over low heat and stir until very warm. Drizzle the glaze over the cooled cake. Arrange pecan halves in a pattern of your choice on the top.

GINGER'S CHEESE CAKE

Serves 10

Crust
1 1/2 cups graham cracker crumbs (21 crackers)
1/3 cup sugar
1/2 cup melted butter

Cake
2 pounds cream cheese, softened
1 cup sugar
1/4 teaspoon ground cinnamon
1 teaspoon vanilla extract
2 teaspoons grated lemon rind
2 tablespoons fresh lemon juice
4 eggs, separated

Topping
12 ounces sour cream
1 1/2 tablespoons sugar
1 1/2 teaspoons vanilla extract

Heat oven to 300°

Crust: Blend crumbs, butter and sugar. Press into bottom of well-buttered 9-inch springform pan. Bake 5 minutes. Cool.

Cake: Blend cream cheese with sugar, cinnamon, vanilla, lemon rind and lemon juice. Beat in egg yolks one at a time. Beat egg whites until stiff and fold into cheese mixture. Pour mixture on top of crumbs. Bake 35 minutes.

Topping: Blend sour cream, sugar and vanilla. Spread on baked cake. Bake 10 more minutes, until golden brown. Cool to room temperature. Refrigerate.

DESSERTS

NEW YORK CHEESE CAKE

Serves 16

5 (8-ounce) packages cream cheese
1/2 cup (1 stick) butter
12 ounces sour cream
2 tablespoons cornstarch
1 cup sugar
1 teaspoon vanilla extract
1 tablespoon lemon juice
5 large eggs

Heat oven to 350°

Allow first 3 ingredients to reach room temperature.

Combine cream cheese, butter and sour cream. Mix well. Add cornstarch, sugar, vanilla and lemon juice and beat at high speed with electric mixer until well blended. Continue beating while adding 1 egg at a time.

Pour into greased large (101/2-to 11-inch) springform pan and place into large pan of warm water filled half way up springform pan. Bake about 50 minutes, until light brown on top. Turn oven off and leave cake in oven with door slightly ajar for 45 minutes.

Cool on stove another 45 minutes and refrigerate.

CHART HOUSE MUD PIE

Serves 8

This famous recipe comes from the Chart House Restaurant.

1/2 package chocolate wafers
1/4 cup (1/2 stick) butter, melted
1 gallon coffee ice cream, softened
1 1/2 cups fudge sauce

Crush wafers and add butter. Mix well. Press into a deep-dish 9-inch pie plate. Cover with soft coffee ice cream. Top with cold fudge sauce. (It helps to place fudge sauce in the freezer for a while to make spreading easier.) Freeze for approximately 10 hours.

To serve: Slice the Mud Pie into eight portions and serve on chilled dessert plates. Top with whipped cream and diced almonds.

CHOCOLATE DELUXE PECAN PIE

Serves 8

4 squares (1 ounce each) semi-sweet chocolate
2 tablespoons butter or margarine
3 eggs, lightly beaten
1 cup light corn syrup
1 cup sugar
1 teaspoon vanilla extract
1 to 1 1/2 cups chopped pecans
1 unbaked 9-inch pie shell

Heat oven to 350°

Melt chocolate and butter in saucepan. In a large bowl, stir eggs, corn syrup, sugar and vanilla until well blended. Add chocolate to butter mixture; stir. Blend in pecans. Pour into pie shell. Bake for 50 - 55 minutes, or until knife inserted halfway between center and edge comes out clean.

For plain Pecan Pie do not add chocolate.

MISSISSIPPI MINT PIE

Serves 8

The crust uses about 3/4 of an 8 1/2-ounce box of chocolate wafers.

Pie
1 1/2 *cups chocolate wafer crumbs*
6 tablespoons (3/4 stick) unsalted butter, melted
2 tablespoons clear Crème de Menthe liqueur
1 quart vanilla ice cream, softened
1 1/2 *quarts chocolate ice cream, softened*

Sauce
1 tablespoon cornstarch
1/4 cup milk
1/4 cup whipping cream
3 ounces unsweetened chocolate, coarsely chopped
6 tablespoons (3/4 stick) unsalted butter
1/2 cup sugar
1 teaspoon vanilla

Pie: Combine crumbs and butter in 9-inch pie pan; press mixture into bottom and sides. Freeze crust until firm.

Line an 8-inch metal bowl with plastic wrap, allowing overhang. Stir Crème de Menthe into vanilla ice cream. Pack into prepared bowl. Spread chocolate ice cream in pie crust. Freeze bowl and crust until ice cream is firm.

Sauce: Whisk cornstarch into milk in small bowl. Whisk in cream. Melt chocolate and butter with sugar in small heavy saucepan over low heat, stirring until smooth. Whisk cornstarch mixture into chocolate. Reduce heat and whisk until mixture thickens. Remove from heat. Stir in vanilla. Cool to room temperature.

NO-EGG CHOCOLATE PUDDING PIE

Serves 6

1 cup sugar
5 tablespoons flour
5 tablespoons unsweetened cocoa
2 1/2 cups boiling water
1 1/2 teaspoons vanilla extract
1 tablespoon butter or margarine (optional)
1 8-inch graham-cracker pie crust

Mix first 3 ingredients in medium-size saucepan. Add water, vanilla and butter and cook until boiling, stirring constantly with a wire whisk.

Pour into crust and cool.

BUTTERMILK PIE

Serves 8

4 tablespoons flour
1 cup sugar
1/3 cup butter, softened
4 large eggs, beaten
2 tablespoons lemon juice
1 tablespoon grated lemon rind
2 cups buttermilk
9-inch deep-dish pie crust

Heat oven to 450°

Mix flour and sugar. Cream with butter. Add eggs, lemon juice and rind. Stir until well mixed. Add buttermilk and stir. Pour into pie shell and bake for 15 minutes. Then reduce heat to 350° and bake for 30 minutes more, or until firm. Cool on rack.

DESSERTS

LORETTA'S FLAPPER PIE

Serves 6 to 8

Custard pie in a graham-cracker crust with meringue topping.

Crust
12 single graham crackers
6 tablespoons (3/4 stick) butter or margarine, softened
3 tablespoons sugar

Custard
3 egg yolks
1/4 cup sugar
1/8 teaspoon salt
1/2 teaspoon vanilla extract
2 cups scalded milk

Meringue
2 egg whites
2 tablespoons sugar
1/4 teaspoon vanilla extract

Heat oven to 375°

Crust: Combine all ingredients, mixing until blended. Press firmly into a 9-inch pie plate. Bake for 8 minutes. Cool.

Custard: Beat egg yolks slightly with a fork. Add sugar, salt and vanilla; stir. Gradually add milk, stirring continuously. Cook mixture for 15 to 20 minutes over boiling water in double boiler until thickened. (If the custard is still too loose, add 1/4 cup of cornstarch to thicken.) Place a fork into mixture; if coating sticks to the fork, the custard is done. Remove from the heat immediately. Cool slightly and pour into prepared pie crust.

Meringue: Beat egg whites until stiff peaks form. Add sugar gradually, 1/2 tablespoon at a time. Stir in vanilla. Beat mixture until peaks form again. Top custard with meringue and add any remaining graham-cracker crumbs. Bake for 15 minutes, or until meringue is slightly browned. Cool.

210

KEY LIME PIE

Yield: 1 9-inch pie

4 eggs, separated
1 14-ounce can sweetened condensed milk
1/2 cup lime juice
1 9-inch pie crust, baked

Meringue
3 egg whites
1/4 teaspoon cream of tartar
1/3 cup sugar

Beat the 4 egg yolks and the white of 1 egg until thick. Add the condensed milk and beat again. Then add the lime juice and beat until thick. Beat the remaining egg whites separately until they are dry, and fold them into the mixture. Pour the mixture into pie shell and chill.

Heat oven to 425°.

Meringue: Beat the remaining 3 egg whites until they are dry and frothy. Add the cream of tartar and beat again until the whites form a peak. Slowly beat in the sugar, and continue beating until the meringue becomes stiff and shiny. Spread the meringue over the cooled pie filling. Bake for 5 minutes, or until the meringue turns brown. Cool.

SHOOFLY PIE

Yield: 1 9-inch pie

This is an old Kentucky recipe.

3/4 cup dark molasses
3/4 cup hot water
1/2 teaspoon baking soda
1 1/2 cups flour
1/2 cup brown or maple sugar
1/4 cup (4 tablespoons) butter
1 9-inch pie crust, unbaked

Heat oven to 375°

In a bowl, mix the molasses with the hot water and blend them together well. (The hotter the water, the easier it will be to mix.) In a separate bowl, blend the baking soda, flour, sugar and butter into a grainy crumble.

Put the pastry in the pie dish. Pour in one-third of the molasses mixture, then one-third of the crumb mixture, repeating this alternation until you end up with the crumbs on top. Bake for 35 minutes. Cool.

WHITE-RUSSIAN MOUSSE PIE

Serves 8 to 10

This is a decadently delicious adult dessert.

Crust
11/2 cups chocolate-wafer cookie crumbs (about 30 wafers)
1/4 cup (1/2 stick) butter, melted
2 tablespoons sugar

Filling
1 envelope unflavored gelatin
1/4 cup cold water
3 eggs, separated
7 tablespoons sugar
1/4 cup plus 1 tablespoon Kahlúa liqueur
2 tablespoons vodka
1/2 cup heavy cream

Topping
1 cup heavy cream
3 tablespoons Kahlúa liqueur
2 tablespoons sugar

Garnish: White and dark chocolate curls (optional)

Crust: Combine ingredients. Place in a 9-inch springform pan; press into bottom and up sides. Refrigerate until firm.

Filling: Sprinkle gelatin over water in a small bowl. Set in pan of simmering water and stir until dissolved. Whisk yolks and 4 tablespoons sugar in large bowl until thick and light. Gradually whisk in dissolved gelatin. Blend in Kahlúa and vodka. Set in large bowl filled with ice and stir until mixture thickens, about 5 minutes.

Beat whites to soft peaks. Gradually add remaining 3 tablespoons sugar and beat until stiff and shiny. Fold into gelatin mixture. Beat 1/2 cup cream to stiff peaks. Fold into gelatin mixture. Turn filling into crust. Refrigerate pie at least 3 hours or overnight.

Topping: Beat cream to soft peaks. Add Kahlúa and sugar and beat to stiff peaks. Swirl topping over pie. Garnish with chocolate curls if desired. Serve chilled.

VIENNESE APPLE STRUDEL

Serves 12

1/2 cup dark raisins
3 tablespoons brandy
2 cups (2 medium) thinly sliced Granny Smith apples,
*   peeled and cored*
1/2 cup chopped walnuts
2 tablespoons sugar
2 tablespoons butter, softened
1 tablespoon grated lemon peel
1/2 teaspoon ground cinnamon
1/2 teaspoon vanilla extract
2 tablespoons butter
1/2 cup bread crumbs
1/2 cup apricot preserves
6 sheets fillo dough
3 tablespoons butter, softened
Confectioners sugar to dust

In a large bowl, soak raisins in 1 tablespoon brandy for 2 hours. Add apples, walnuts, sugar, 2 tablespoons butter, lemon peel, cinnamon and vanilla. Mix well and set aside.

In a small skillet over medium heat, melt 2 tablespoons butter and stir in bread crumbs. Cook about 2 minutes, or until lightly browned.

In a small saucepan over low heat, melt apricot preserves and stir in remaining tablespoon of brandy.

Prepare 1 large fillo strudel. Spread warm apricot mixture on top fillo sheet and sprinkle with bread crumbs. Spread with apple mixture and roll. Score top into 12 equal sections.

Heat oven to 350°

Bake on greased baking sheet for 45 to 50 minutes, or until golden brown. Cool. Dust with confectioners sugar.

BANANAS FOSTER

Serves 6

A New Orleans specialty. Ice cream does best if scooped into balls and frozen ahead of time and bowls are chilled so both are very cold when Bananas Foster is ready to serve.

5 bananas - very firm
1/2 cup (1 stick) unsalted butter
1 cup dark brown sugar
1/2 teaspoon ground cinnamon (optional)
1 teaspoon vanilla extract
1/2 cup banana liqueur
1/2 cup rum

Slice each banana in three slices lengthwise, then cut in halves; set aside. Melt the butter in a large skillet. Add brown sugar and cinnamon, if desired, and cook over low heat, stirring into a thick paste. Add vanilla and banana liqueur and stir well. Cook about 3 minutes. Add banana slices and cook over medium heat, basting well with the sugar-and-butter mixture. Cook about 5 minutes. (Mixture will bubble while cooking.)

Heat the rum in a small saucepan or metal cup; ignite, and pour over bananas. (Rum will have a faint blue flame in cup and will flame up when poured over the bananas.) Stir well to blend, then serve mixture with pieces of bananas over vanilla ice cream.

BREAD PUDDING WITH AMARETTO SAUCE

Serves 8

A New Orleans favorite.

Pudding
1 loaf stale French bread
1 quart milk
1/2 cup sugar
6 eggs, beaten
1 cup raisins
1 tablespoon vanilla extract
Splash Amaretto

Sauce
1 stick unsalted butter
1 cup confectioners sugar
1/4 cup Amaretto (or other liqueur)
1 egg yolk

Heat oven to 375°

Pudding: Tear bread into pieces. In a large bowl, soak bread in milk. Add sugar, raisins, vanilla and eggs. Mix very lightly. Place in well-buttered baking dish. Bake approximately 30 minutes.

Sauce: Over low heat, melt butter and sugar together, stirring constantly. Add Amaretto and egg yolk. Heat slowly for 1 or 2 minutes to set eggs. Pour sauce over bread pudding.

ALL-AMERICAN CHOCOLATE BROWNIES

Yield: 16

Part truffle and part cake, these are best several hours after baking.

1 cup (2 sticks) unsalted butter
3 ounces unsweetened chocolate, coarsely chopped
1/2 cup plus 1 tablespoon all-purpose flour, sifted
1/2 teaspoon baking soda
2 eggs, room temperature
1/4 teaspoon salt
1 cup sugar
2 tablespoons orange liqueur, such as Grand Marnier or Cointreau
1 teaspoon vanilla extract
1 6-ounce package semi-sweet chocolate chips
1 cup chopped walnuts
Sugar

Heat oven to 350°

Position rack in center of oven. Grease an 8-inch square baking pan. Line with parchment, extending paper 1 inch above pan sides. Grease paper generously; dust with sugar.

Melt butter and unsweetened chocolate in top of double boiler over barely simmering water. Stir until smooth. Remove from over water. Sift flour and baking soda together. Using electric mixer, beat eggs and salt until lemon colored. Gradually add 1 cup sugar and beat until mixture is pale yellow and a slowly dissolving ribbon forms when beaters are lifted.

Blend in chocolate mixture, then liqueur and vanilla. Stir in flour. Fold in chocolate chips and walnuts. Pour batter into prepared pan, spreading evenly. Bake until top is firm but center is soft, 20 to 22 minutes. Sprinkle top with sugar. Cool in pan on rack.

Remove brownies from pan using parchment as aid. Cut into 2-inch squares using serrated knife.

CHOCOLATE TORTE WITH APRICOT FILLING

Serves 10

Cake
6 large eggs
3/4 cup minus 1 tablespoon sugar
1 teaspoon vanilla extract
1/2 cup plus 1 tablespoon sifted all-purpose flour
1/2 cup sifted unsweetened cocoa
1 teaspoon ground allspice
1 teaspoon ground cinnamon
1/4 teaspoon ground nutmeg

Frosting and Filling
11/2 cups part-skim ricotta cheese
1/4 cup plus 2 tablespoons unsweetened cocoa
2 tablespoons instant espresso powder
3 tablespoons sugar
2 teaspoons vanilla extract
1/8 teaspoon salt
3/4 cup apricot all-fruit spread

Garnish: Strawberries

Heat oven to 350°

Cake: Spray two 8-inch round cake pans with nonstick cooking spray. In a large bowl, using an electric mixer set at high speed, beat the eggs, sugar, and vanilla until thick and tripled in volume, about 7 minutes.

In a medium bowl, sift together the flour, cocoa powder, allspice, cinnamon, and nutmeg. Using a large rubber spatula, quickly and gently fold the dry ingredients into the egg mixture, until smooth. Divide the mixture between the two prepared pans. Bake until a toothpick inserted in the center comes out clean, about 15 minutes. Cool completely in the pans set on racks.

Frosting: In a food processor or blender, process the ricotta cheese, cocoa powder, espresso powder, sugar, vanilla and salt until smooth. Cover and chill the frosting until ready to use.

When the cake is cool, turn it out of the pans. With a long serrated knife, split each layer in half horizontally and spread the bottom of each layer with half of the apricot all-fruit spread. Carefully replace the top halves.

Spread half of the frosting evenly over the top of one of the filled layers. Stack the second filled layer on top of the first. Swirl the remaining frosting evenly over the top of the cake. Garnish with whole strawberries, if desired.

218

DEEP CHOCOLATE

Serves 20

A chocolate lover's delight. For sweeter palates, use 2 pounds dark sweet chocolate instead of mixing with semi-sweet.

1 pound dark sweet chocolate, cut into pieces
1 pound semi-sweet chocolate, cut into pieces
6 ounces (11/2 sticks) butter, cut into pieces
1 cup sifted confectioners sugar
6 large eggs, separated
1/4 cup rum
1/4 cup crème de cacao
2 teaspoons instant coffee powder
4 cups (1 quart) heavy cream

Garnish: Whipped cream

Melt chocolate and butter in top of double boiler set over simmering water. Combine sugar, yolks, rum, crème de cacao, and coffee in a large mixing bowl. Blend into chocolate mixture.

Whip the 4 cups heavy cream in a very large bowl until stiff peaks form. Gently fold whipped cream into chocolate mixture, blending thoroughly.

Beat egg whites until soft peaks form. Fold egg whites into chocolate cream. Turn mixture into 10-to 11-inch springform pan, filling to top. Refrigerate overnight. Transfer pan to chilled platter and remove springform.

Garnish with whipped cream and serve. This recipe can be halved.

DEVIL DOGS

Yield: 12

Cake
1/2 cup (1 stick) butter or margarine, softened
1 cup sugar
1 egg
1 cup milk
1 teaspoon vanilla extract
2 cups all-purpose flour
11/2 teaspoons baking soda
1/2 teaspoon baking powder
1/2 cup unsweetened cocoa
1/2 teaspoon salt

Filling
1/2 cup shortening
1 cup confectioners sugar
1 cup marshmallow fluff
1/2 teaspoon vanilla extract

Heat oven to 425°

Cake: Cream butter and sugar in a large bowl with electric mixer; add egg, milk, and vanilla and blend until thoroughly mixed. Add all dry ingredients in order listed, to liquid mixture, and beat on medium speed for 2 minutes scraping down sides of mixing bowl often.

Drop by rounded teaspoon onto ungreased cookie sheet. Bake 7 minutes. Remove from cookie sheet and cool on brown paper bag.

Filling: Blend all ingredients together until creamy; add a few drops of milk, if necessary, to make mixture spreadable. Spread between two chocolate cakes and put together to make a sandwich.

HEAVENLY CHOCOLATE ROLL

Serves 6 to 8

Cake
3 large eggs, separated
6 tablespoons sugar
4 tablespoons unsweetened cocoa
1 tablespoon vanilla extract

Filling
1 1/2 cups heavy cream
1/4 cup sugar
2 tablespoons unsweetened cocoa
1/2 teaspoon vanilla extract

Heat oven to 350°

Grease a 9 x 15-inch jelly-roll pan and line with waxed paper.

Cake: Beat egg yolks in a large bowl with electric mixer. Add 5 tablespoons sugar gradually, and continue beating until mixture is creamy. Stir in 3 tablespoons of cocoa and vanilla. Beat egg whites in a small bowl until stiff and gently mix into cocoa mixture. Pour into pan and smooth top to make batter even. Bake 10 minutes, or until toothpick inserted in center comes out clean. (Cake is very thin, so be carefull that edges don't get hard.)

Spread two sheets of plastic wrap, overlapping them to make a rectangle larger than the cake. Sprinkle the plastic wrap all over with mixture of 1 tablespoon cocoa and 1 tablespoon sugar. When the cake has cooled for 5 minutes, turn it out onto the plastic, trying to center it so that you will have several inches of plastic wrap on all sides. Peel off waxed paper. Roll up cake, using plastic wrap to move, but do not have plastic wrap inside of the roll. You may have to cut off some edges of the cake if they get too hard to roll.

Filling: Mix, do not whip, cream, sugar, cocoa and vanilla in small bowl. Refrigerate, covered, for several hours or overnight. When ready to fill cake, whip mixture until it holds its shape. Unroll cake and spread filling evenly, saving some of the filling to use on top. Roll up cake with filling, and cover with remaining filling.

DESSERTS

PARCEL TORTE

Serves 8 to 10

Unusual dessert, a chocolate lover's delight!

7 squares (1 ounce each) semi-sweet chocolate, cut up
1/2 cup (1 stick) butter
1 cup sugar
7 large eggs, separated

Garnish: Chocolate shavings
*   Whipped cream*

Heat oven to 325°

Melt the chocolate and butter over boiling water in a double boiler over low heat. Add 3/4 cup of the sugar and egg yolks; beat for 3 minutes at high speed.

In a large bowl, beat egg whites until soft peaks form. Add remaining 1/4 cup sugar gradually, beating constantly until whites hold their peaks. Fold egg whites slowly into the chocolate batter with a rubber spatula.

Pour only three-fourths of the batter into an ungreased 9-inch springform pan. Bake for 35 minutes. Let torte cool and fall. Then run knife around edge and remove frame. Pour the remaining uncooked batter over the top and chill.

Garnish with chocolate shavings and whipped cream.

HOLIDAY CHOCOLATE LOG

Serves 10

You may make the Chocolate Log a week ahead, then freeze it wrapped in foil. Let stand at room temperature to thaw for about 1 hour before serving.

Log
6 egg whites, room temperature
3/4 cup granulated sugar
6 egg yolks
1/3 cup unsweetened cocoa
1 1/2 teaspoons vanilla extract
Dash salt
Confectioners sugar

Filling
1 1/2 cups heavy cream
1/3 cup confectioners sugar
1/4 cup unsweetened cocoa
2 teaspoons instant coffee
1 teaspoon vanilla extract

Garnish: Candied cherries angelica

Heat oven to 375°

Grease bottom of a 15 1/2 x 10 1/2 x 1-inch jelly-roll pan; line with waxed paper; grease lightly. In a large electric mixer bowl, at high speed, beat egg whites just until soft peaks form when the beater is slowly raised.

Add 1/4 cup sugar, 2 tablespoons at a time, beating until stiff peaks form when beater is slowly raised. With same beaters, beat yolks at high speed, adding remaining 1/2 cup sugar, 2 tablespoons at a time. Beat until mixture is very thick, about 4 minutes.

At low speed, beat in cocoa, vanilla and salt, just until smooth. With wire whisk or rubber scraper, using an under-and-over motion, gently fold the cocoa mixture into the beaten egg whites, just until they are blended (no egg white should show).

Spread evenly in pan. Bake 15 minutes, just until surface springs back when gently pressed with fingertip. Sift confectioners sugar onto a 15 x 10-inch piece of waxed paper, and put on a clean linen towel. Turn cake out on sugar; lift off pan; peel paper off cake. (Continued on Page 224.)

223

HOLIDAY CHOCOLATE LOG (cont'd)

Roll up, jelly-roll fashion, starting with the short end, towel and all. Cool completely on rack, seam side down, at least 1/2 hour.

Filling: Combine ingredients in medium bowl. Beat with electric mixer until thick, and then refrigerate.

Unroll cake; spread with filling to 1 inch from edge; reroll. Place, seam side down, on plate; cover loosely with foil. Refrigerate 1 hour before serving.

To serve: Sprinkle with confectioners' sugar; decorate with angelica and cherries.

CRÈME BRÛLÈE

Serves 8

1 quart heavy cream
3/4 cup granulated sugar
10 egg yolks
2 teaspoons vanilla extract
Sugar in the raw (a coarse light brown sugar)

Heat oven to 275°

Scald cream and half the granulated sugar, remove from heat. Whisk together yolks, remaining granulated sugar and vanilla, and combine with the cream. Pass through a fine strainer. Ladle the preparation into 8 ceramic custard cups (6 ounces each) and place in a shallow roasting pan.

Carefully pour into the pan enough hot water to reach halfway up the sides of the cups. Bake for about 1 hour, or until custard has set. (Times will vary with each oven.) Chill cooked creams.

To serve, sprinkle with sugar in the raw and place under a hot broiler until surface is browned.

DESSERTS

CREAM PUFFS

Yield: 50

Puffs can be prepared 1 week ahead. Wrap tightly and freeze. Thaw, then recrisp in 300° oven for 5 minutes.

Puffs
1 cup hot water
1/2 cup (1 stick) butter
1/8 teaspoon salt
1 cup all-purpose flour
2 teaspoons sugar
4 eggs

Filling
1 package vanilla pudding
1 cup milk
1 cup heavy cream
1 teaspoon vanilla extract

Heat oven to 450°

Puffs: Melt butter in water with salt in medium saucepan. Bring to a boil. Remove from heat and add flour and sugar. Stir continuously until mixture forms a ball or leaves sides of pan. Transfer to blender or processor and add eggs, 1 at a time, until well blended.

Drop onto cookie sheet forming 1 1/2 inch balls, and bake until golden, about 15 minutes. Turn oven off and leave in for 10 minutes. Take out and transfer to racks. Slice in half horizontally. Cool.

Filling: Cook pudding as directed with 1 cup milk until thick. Cool. Meanwhile, whip cream with sugar and vanilla until stiff peaks form. Fold pudding into whipped cream and fill cooled puffs.

225

CHOCOLATE MERINGUE COOKIES

Yield: About 36

1 cup (6 ounces) semi-sweet chocolate chips
2 egg whites from large eggs
1/2 cup sugar
1/2 teaspoon vanilla extract
1/2 teaspoon white vinegar
3/4 cup chopped nuts (optional)

Heat oven to 350°

Melt chocolate chips over hot water in double boiler. Beat egg whites until foamy. Gradually add sugar while continuing to beat egg whites, beating until stiff. Beat in vanilla and vinegar. Fold in chocolate and nuts.

Grease cookie sheet and cover with waxed paper. Drop batter, a teaspoon at a time, on sheet, leaving 3 inches between each. Bake for 10 minutes or until firm to the touch. Remove immediately from sheet.

Store in airtight container.

DIETERS' PECAN KISSES

Yield: 25 kisses

This recipe is wheat and milk free and low in cholesterol. You can substitute cashews, walnuts, peanuts or chocolate chips for pecans.

3 egg whites
1/4 teaspoon vanilla extract
1/8 teaspoon salt
1 cup superfine sugar
1 1/2 cups chopped pecans

Heat oven to 325°

Beat egg whites with vanilla and salt until soft peaks form. Gradually beat in sugar, beating until stiff. Fold in pecans. Drop dough by rounded teaspoon onto waxed paper-covered cookie sheets. Bake for about 20 minutes. Remove cookies immediately. Cool.

LOW-FAT CHOCOLATE COOKIES

Yield: 45 cookies

2 cups all-purpose flour
1/2 cup unsweetened cocoa
1/2 teaspoon baking soda
1/3 cup olive oil
2 large egg whites
1/2 cup sugar
1/2 teaspoon vanilla extract

Heat oven to 375°

Sift flour, cocoa and baking soda in a mixing bowl. In a separate bowl, beat oil, egg whites, sugar and vanilla. Add flour mixture to egg mixture and mix well.

Roll dough about 1/4 inch thick and cut out cookies with a cookie cutter. Bake approximately 15 minutes.

NUT CAKES

Yield: 24 using 2 tins

Dough
3 ounces cream cheese, softened
1/4 pound butter or margarine, softened
1 cup sifted flour

Filling
1 egg
3/4 cup brown sugar
1 tablespoon butter or margarine
1 teaspoon vanilla extract
Dash salt
6 ounces pecan halves

Blend cream cheese, butter and flour to make dough. Refrigerate for one hour. Make 24 one inch balls from dough. Place ball in each section of an ungreased miniature muffin tin and press dough into bottom.

Heat oven to 350°.

Chop nuts, saving 24 for later. Beat together eggs, sugar, one tablespoon butter, vanilla and salt until smooth. Fill cups with chopped nuts and then pour egg mixture over nuts. Top with pecan halves. Bake approximately 25 minutes. Remove cakes from tins immediately.

SHORTBREAD SQUARES

Yield: 20 Squares

1 pound (4 sticks) butter, softened
8 ounces confectioners sugar
1 teaspoon vanilla extract
1 teaspoon salt
16 ounces all-purpose flour
8 ounces cornstarch

Heat oven to 300°

Cream butter and sugar. Add vanilla and salt. In separate bowl, mix flour and cornstarch. Gradually add to butter mixture.

Roll dough out to 1/2-inch thickness, and cut into squares. Place on greased cookie sheet. Bake for 30 minutes, or until firm and lightly browned.

BUTTER CRESCENTS

Yield: About 60

1/2 pound (2 sticks) butter, softened
4 tablespoons superfine or confectioners sugar
2 cups flour
1 tablespoon cold water
1 teaspoon vanilla extract
1 cup finely chopped pecans or walnuts
1/2 teaspoon salt

Heat oven to 375°

On flat board or in a bowl, combine all ingredients and mix with fingers. Roll dough into thin strips 1 1/2 inches long and form into crescent shapes. Bake on an ungreased cookie sheet until lightly browned approximately 20 minutes. Remove from pan and cool. Roll in superfine sugar or dust with confectioners sugar.

DESSERTS

PUMPKIN BARS

Bars
4 eggs
1 cup oil
2 cups sugar
1 1/2 cups all-purpose flour
1 teaspoon baking soda
1 teaspoon salt
2 teaspoons ground cinnamon
2 cups canned solid-pack pumpkin

Frosting
3 ounces cream cheese, softened
1/2 cup (1 stick) butter or margarine, softened
2 cups confectioners sugar
1 teaspoon vanilla extract

Heat oven to 350°

Bars: Mix the eggs, oil and sugar in a large mixing bowl with an electric beater until well blended. Add remaining dry ingredients and mix well. Blend in pumpkin on low speed until thoroughly mixed. Pour into greased jelly-roll pan. Bake for 30-40 minutes. Cool.

Frosting: Blend cream cheese and butter in medium-size mixing bowl with electric beater until mixed. Add confectioners sugar and vanilla and blend until creamy. Spread on cake before cutting into bars.

ROCKY-ROAD SQUARES

Yield: 20

1 12-ounce package milk-chocolate chips
1 14-ounce can sweetened condensed milk
2 tablespoons butter or margarine
2 cups pecans, chopped
1 10 1/2-ounce package mini marshmallows

In top of double boiler, combine chocolate chips, milk and butter. Cook over boiling water until ingredients are melted and well blended. Stir occasionally.

In a large bowl, combine nuts and marshmallows. Fold in chocolate mixture.

Line a 13 x 9-inch pan with waxed paper. Spread mixture over paper. Chill 2 hours, or until firm. Remove from pan; peel off paper; cut into squares.

Store in an airtight container at room temperature.

DESSERTS

TASSIES

Yield: 48 (using 4 pans)

Dough
6 ounces cream cheese, softened
1/2 pound (2 sticks) unsalted butter, softened
2 cups sifted flour

Filling
3 eggs, slightly beaten
1 1/2 cups brown sugar
3 tablespoons butter, melted
1 teaspoon vanilla extract
1 cup chopped walnuts
Confectioners sugar

Dough: Mix dough ingredients and form into 1-inch balls. Place one in each section of an ungreased tassie tin. Press dough with fingers against sides of tray to form a tart like pastry.

Heat oven to 350°

Filling: Combine all filling ingredients and mix well. Fill each section of dough 3/4 inch full. Bake for approximately 25 to 30 minutes, or until golden brown. Cool and remove from tins. Sprinkle with confectioners sugar.

NO-BAKE ALMOND SNOWBALLS

Yield: About 30

1/2 cup (1 stick) butter
4 squares (4 ounces) semi-sweet chocolate
1 teaspoon vanilla extract
1 cup finely ground almonds (process almonds in a blender or
*   food processor until very fine)*
1 cup unsweetened coconut, plus extra for coating balls
1 cup toasted slivered almonds
3 tablespoons honey
1/8 teaspoon salt
1/2 cup wheat germ

Melt the butter and chocolate over hot water or very low heat. Stir in the vanilla.

In a bowl, combine the ground almonds, 1 cup unsweetened coconut, toasted slivered almonds, honey, salt and wheat germ. Stir in the melted butter mixture. Chill the mixture until it is firm enough to mold into balls.

Form the mixture into 1-inch balls and roll in unsweetened coconut. Set on a tray and chill until firm.

DESSERTS

LEMON BREAD

Yield: 2 loaves

Lemon Bread is delicious with a dollop of whipped cream.

3 cups all-purpose flour
1 teaspoon baking soda
1 teaspoon salt
1/2 teaspoon baking powder
3 eggs
13/4 cups granulated sugar
1 cup vegetable oil
2 cartons vanilla yogurt (8 ounces each)
1 teaspoon lemon extract

Sift together flour, baking soda, salt and baking powder. Set aside.

Heat oven to 325°

Break eggs into large mixing bowl; beat until foamy. Add sugar and oil; beat about 1 minute more. Add yogurt and lemon extract; beat about 1 minute. Add flour mixture to egg mixture; beat until very smooth.

Pour batter into 2 greased and floured 9 x 5 x 3-inch loaf pans. Fill pans about half full; batter will rise to top during baking. Tap pans to release air bubbles. Smooth top of batter. Bake for 45 minutes to 1 hour, or until toothpick inserted in center comes out clean and top of loaf is a nice golden brown.

Let loaves cool in pan or on rack, and then carefully remove loaves from pans.

RASPBERRY TART

1/2 cup ground almonds
3 tablespoons sugar
10 sheets fillo dough
1/2 cup (1 stick) butter, softened
1/2 cup almond paste
2 large eggs, lightly beaten
2 teaspoons flour
1 1/2 pints raspberries
1/2 cup raspberry jelly, heated to a liquid

Heat oven to 400°

In a small bowl, combine almonds and sugar. Cut fillo into 12-inch circles. Using 1/4 cup of the butter in 10-inch tart pan with removable bottom, brush each circle with butter, then sprinkle almond/sugar mixture over butter. Repeat process until all fillo circles are utilized.

In medium bowl, combine remaining 1/4 cup butter, almond paste, eggs and flour. Using an electric mixer, beat at high speed until smooth. Spread butter mixture on fillo crust and bake in oven for 20 to 25 minutes, or until golden brown.

Remove tart from oven and arrange raspberries on fillo. Brush with heated jelly. Serve warm or chilled, with ice cream or whipped cream.

DESSERTS

STRAWBERRY-CHEESECAKE TRIFLE

Serves 24

2 (8 ounce) packages cream cheese, room temperature
2 cups confectioners sugar
1 cup sour cream
1 1/2 teaspoons vanilla extract
3/4 teaspoon almond extract
1 cup whipping cream
4 tablespoons granulated sugar
1 large angel food cake, torn into pieces
2 quarts strawberries, hulled, washed and thinly sliced

In a large bowl, blend cream cheese and confectioners sugar; add sour cream, 1/2 teaspoon vanilla extract and 1/4 teaspoon almond extract. Set aside.

In a small deep bowl, whip cream, 1 teaspoon vanilla extract and 1 table-spoon granulated sugar. Fold whipped cream into cream cheese mixture. Add cake pieces and set aside.

Combine strawberries, 3 tablespoons granulated sugar and 1/2 teaspoon almond extract. In a large glass bowl, (trifle bowl, if you have one), spread a layer of strawberries, then cake mixture. Continue layering, finishing with strawberries. Cover with plastic wrap and chill well.

CHOCOLATE MOUSSE RAPHAEL

Serves 6 to 8

1 square (1 ounce) unsweetened chocolate
11/2 teaspoons unsweetened cocoa
3 tablespoons hot, strong brewed coffee
2 egg yolks
21/2 cups heavy cream
2 tablespoons Grand Marnier or other orange liqueur
1 tablespoon Kahlúa or other coffee liqueur
1 tablespoon crème de cacao
1 cup sifted confectioners sugar

Garnish: 1 cup whipped cream
*   Chocolate curls (optional)*

In the top part of a double boiler over hot (not boiling) water, or in a heavy 1-quart saucepan, melt chocolate. Remove pan from heat. Stir in cocoa powder to form a smooth paste. Add coffee and stir until smooth. Set aside.

In a small bowl, beat egg yolks and 1/2 cup heavy cream. Gradually stir about half of chocolate mixture into yolks. Reutrn all to double boiler or saucepan. Cook over medium-low heat until mixture thickens. Do not boil.

Remove the saucepan from the heat. Stir in the Grand Marnier, the Kahlúa and the crème de cacao. Beat in the confectioners sugar until mixture is smooth. Cool to room temperature.

In a large, chilled bowl, whip the remaining 2 cups heavy cream with an electric mixer or processor until soft peaks form (tips curl). Fold in the chocolate mixture. Cover and refrigerate the mousse for 3 to 4 hours.

To serve, spoon the chocolate mousse into 6 to 8 dessert dishes. Spoon extra whipped cream onto each serving. Sprinkle with chocolate curls.

DESSERTS

LEMON MOUSSE WITH RASPBERRY SAUCE

Serves 8 to 10

This mousse is rich and intense, so small portions, lavished with raspberry purée, will satisfy every lemon lover in the crowd. You can present this mousse in a large bowl instead of individual glasses, although it will take an additional 3 hours to set.

6 large eggs
6 large egg yolks
11/2 cups plus 2 tablespoons sugar
1 cup fresh lemon juice, strained
2 tablespoons minced lemon peel
14 tablespoons (13/4 sticks) chilled unsalted butter, cut into small
    pieces
3/4 cup chilled heavy cream
11/2 cups fresh raspberries or frozen, unsweetened, thawed

Whisk eggs and yolks in heavy non aluminum saucepan until foamy. Whisk in 11/2 cups sugar, then lemon juice. Mix in peel. Stir over low heat until mixture thickens to consistency of heavy custard, about 10 minutes; do not boil. Remove from heat and whisk in butter. Transfer mixture to bowl and chill until very thick, stirring occasionally, about 1 hour.

Whip cream in medium bowl to soft peaks. Gently fold cream into lemon mixture. Spoon mousse into individual serving glasses. Cover and refrigerate until set, about 2 hours.

Coarsely mash berries in small bowl using a fork. Mix in 2 tablespoons sugar. Taste, adding more sugar if desired. Cover and refrigerate 1 hour to release juices.

Spoon sauce over center of mousse.

PISTACHIO SOUFFLÉ

Serves 6

1 1/2 tablespoons butter
1/4 cup superfine sugar
1/2 teaspoon unsweetened cocoa
1 1/4 cups milk
2 ounces shelled pistachios
1 whole egg plus 1 egg yolk
1/4 cup granulated sugar
1/3 cup flour
6 egg whites

Heat oven to 450°

Butter six individual soufflé dishes and coat them with a mixture of the superfine sugar and the cocoa. Boil the milk with the pistachios for 10 minutes, or until the nuts are soft. Purée the mixture in a blender or a food processor until it is smooth.

In a small bowl, beat together the eggs, the egg yolk and half the sugar for 2 minutes. Add the flour and mix for 1 minute. Stir in the milk-and-pistachio mixture. Transfer to a bowl, cover it tightly and keep the mixture warm.

In a large bowl, beat the egg whites until they form soft peaks. Add the remaining 1/8 cup sugar and continue beating until the egg whites form stiff peaks. Stir one-fourth of the egg whites into the pistachio mixture to lighten it up, then fold in the remaining egg whites.

Transfer the soufflé mixture to the soufflé dishes, smoothing the tops evenly. Bake the soufflés in the oven for 10 minutes, or until puffed and lightly browned. Serve with vanilla or white pistachio ice cream.

CREAMY STRAWBERRY MOUSSE

Serves 6 to 8

Can be prepared 1 day ahead.

1 pint fresh strawberries, hulled, washed and puréed
2/3 cup sugar
1/4 teaspoon salt
4 tablespoons water
2 teaspoons fresh lemon juice
1 1/4-ounce envelope unflavored gelatin
2 eggs, separated
1/4 cup sugar
1 cup heavy cream

Garnish: Additional whipped cream
6 to 8 strawberries

Stir puréed strawberries, 2/3 cup sugar and salt in medium saucepan over low heat. Heat through. Combine water and lemon juice in small bowl. Sprinkle gelatin over. Set bowl in pan of simmering water and stir until gelatin dissolves. Stir into strawberry mixture. Cool.

Meanwhile, whisk yolks in double boiler over barely simmering water. Add 1/4 cup sugar and cook until thickened and sugar dissolves, whisking constantly, 3 to 4 minutes. Remove from heat. Stir in 1/4 cup strawberry mixture. Add yolk mixture to remaining strawberry mixture. Cool 5 minutes.

Whip the heavy cream and fold into berries. Beat egg whites to soft peaks. Fold into strawberry mixture. Spoon mousse into goblets or serving bowl. Cover and refrigerate. Garnish with additional whipped cream and strawberries.

WARM FRUIT DESSERT TOPPING

Serves 4 to 6

This easy, elegant dessert makes use of kitchen staples and ice cream. Great for unexpected dinner guests. Use whatever fresh fruits are in season.

1 large seedless orange or 2 small tangerines
1 large, cored apple
1 banana
1 small box (a "handful") of raisins
1/4 cup honey
2 tablespoons brown sugar (optional)
1/2 gallon vanilla ice cream
1/2 cup chopped nuts or crunchy whole-grain cereal

Cut fresh fruit in chunks, remove any seeds, and mix in medium saucepan with all but last two ingredients. Cook over low heat about 15 minutes, until warm and bubbly.

Serve warm, over ice cream, and top with either nuts or cereal, as desired.

APRICOT MOLD

Serves 8

48 ounces apricot nectar
2 large packages apricot Jell-O
4 teaspoons vanilla extract

Sauce
1 pint sour cream
2 large jars baby apricot
1 teaspoon vanilla extract

Heat nectar on low heat. Add Jell-O and melt. Add vanilla and pour into 5-cup mold. Chill.

Sauce: Mix all ingredients together and serve on the side.

DESSERTS

TEXAS GRANOLA

8 cups quick-cooking oat meal
1 cup chopped walnuts
1 cup raisins or dried apples
2/3 cup canola oil
2/3 cup honey
2 teaspoons ground cinnamon
1 cup shredded coconut
1/2 teaspoon salt

Heat oven to 350°

Mix all ingredients together. Spread evenly in flat large oblong cookie pan that has been sprayed with nonstick cooking spray.

Bake for 20 minutes, or until granola turns light, golden brown. Cool and store in tightly sealed container in refrigerator. Keeps for several months.

FAST-AND-EASY YOGURT POPS

Makes 10 5-ounce pops

2 (8 ounce) cartons vanilla yogurt
1 (6 ounce) can frozen juice concentrate, thawed
*   (apple, pink lemonade, pineapple or grape)*
10 5-ounce paper cups
10 wooden pop sticks

In a small bowl, combine yogurt and thawed juice. Stir to blend. Fill cups two-thirds full. Place in freezer until partially frozen, about an hour. Insert sticks, freeze. To serve, peel off paper cups. For larger pops, use 5 10-ounce paper cups.

RECIPE CONTRIBUTORS

Helene Aber
Paulette Albera
Rosemary Allen
John Bartalotta
Marilyn Bayer
Joy Benjamin
Judy Benson
Bice Restaurant, New York
Claire Brady
Ginger Busch
Ned Busch
Loretta Carswell
Deborah Channell
Chart House Restaurant, Conn.
Deborah Chase
Chris Clancy
M.H. Cleary
Arlene Cohen
Jean Lahage-Cohen
Ramona Fisher-Collins
Shelly Cooler
M. Day
Nancy Edlin
Nancy Eisenberger
Jackie Favish
Shirley Fawcett
Rhoda Finkelstein
Bridget Flanagan
Rosalie Friedlander
Jeff Gibson
Dorothy Gill
Karen Girosky
Karen Seidler Goodwin
Yvette Goorevitch
Ellen Greene
Lori Greene
Elise Griffin
Nicole Guillemette
Diana Hentel
Chelsay Hiatt
Lindsay Hiatt
Pam Hiatt
Jeff Higgins
Janie Hinkle
Joyce Hoelzer
Kathleen Jacinto
Sharon Jernigan
Linda Keller

Barbara Kempton
Lynda Kieckhefer
Bea King
Beth King
Sheila Kirshner
Gregory S. Kowalzyk
Pat Krayser
Fran Kronick
Susan Lernaya
Lois Linet
Pat Lockhart
Diana Longchamps
Kathy Luzzi
Rosie Magroder
Charlene Marlecka
Maria Monroy
Marina Nadler
Carol Nuba
Tree O'Donnell
Eleanor Pearl
Theresa Penticoff
Elinor Peretsman
Phyllis Perlmutter
Mary & Ron Pohlman
Raphael Restaurant, Mo.
Betty Rashbaum
Buddy Renzullo
Christopher Renzullo
Tina Renzullo
Robin Schlaff
Claire Seidler
Dr. Shelley Sekula
Lucy Seligman
Muriel Seligman
Frances Staebler
Loretta Staebler
Camille Suttle
Reba Tappis
Kathryn Taubert
Tamara Thompson
Leslie Tillema
Joyce Turnipseed
Lydia Valderrama
H.E. Webster
Sally Whitesell
Carol Youngman
Sam Zimmer

243

INDEX

244

INDEX

B (cont'd)

INDEX

D (cont'd)

INDEX

INDEX

L (cont'd)

M

N

O

P

P (cont'd)

INDEX

P (cont'd)

R (cont'd)

S

Salads

Salmon

Sauces

Scallops

INDEX

S (cont'd)

INDEX

256

ORDER FORM

Creative Chef 2
Tourette Syndrome Association, Inc.
42-40 Bell Boulevard
Bayside, NY 11361

Please send ___ copies at . . . .$16.95 each $____
    plus postage & handling. . . . . $ 3.50 each $____
Please send 3 copies at $46.00 plus $6.00 p & h $ 52.00
NYS residents add local sales tax . . . . $____
Enclosed is a check or money order for . . . . $____
(Please make checks payable to TSA-CC2)

Name_____
Address_____
City_____State _____Zip_____

For bulk orders and fundraising projects contact the Fundraising Dept.
(718-224-2999)
Proceeds from the sale of this book support the Tourette Syndrome
Association, Inc.

For shipping outside the USA add $15.00

- -

Creative Chef 2
Tourette Syndrome Association, Inc.
42-40 Bell Boulevard
Bayside, NY 11361

Please send ___ copies at . . . .$16.95 each $____
    plus postage & handling. . . . . $ 3.50 each $____
Please send 3 copies at $46.00 plus $6.00 p & h $ 52.00
NYS residents add local sales tax . . . . $____
Enclosed is a check or money order for . . . . $____
(Please make checks payable to TSA-CC2)

Name_____
Address_____
City_____State _____Zip_____

For bulk orders and fundraising projects contact the Fundraising Dept.
(718-224-2999)
Proceeds from the sale of this book support the Tourette Syndrome
Association, Inc.

For shipping outside the USA add $15.00